COGNITIVE-BEHAVIORAL THERAPY

A Simple Guide to the Skills and Secrets to Help You Overcome Addiction, Manage Anxiety and Depression and Achieve a Positive Mindset Full of Self-Esteem

James Jones

Disclaimer

Table of Contents

Introduction

Cognitive-behavioral therapy is a verbal or coping technique for specific kinds of issues, such as feeding and sleeping illness, psychological disorders, unstable feelings, substance addiction, mental issues, attitude disturbance, and mood problems. CBT uses techniques and systems to tackle various types of behavioral and emotional disorders. For this treatment, there are several approaches used, such as logical-behavioral counseling, dialectical-behavioral therapy, moral-living counseling, reasonable-emotional-behavioral therapy, and cognitive therapy. CBT is a two-way interaction, where the victim gets to share their ideas and emotions as the therapist learns and supports the victim and coaches.

The cognitive model of emotional response, which is cognitive-behavioral therapy, is a great one because its basis is that the thoughts of a person are powerful enough to change their behavior, feelings, and point of view. CBT is known as the type of therapy that delivers great outcomes in a shorter period of time compared to other therapies. CBT is also a time-limited therapy, but it is also an endless process. CBT lets patients do their own tasks and therapies at home. During treatment sessions, the results of the task or assignment are discussed and explained.

Cognitive Model

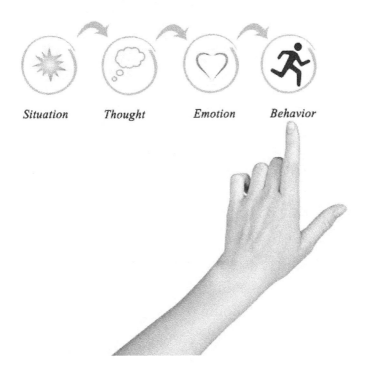

| Situation | Thought | Emotion | Behavior |

Apart from regular therapy sessions, there are many useful professional and self-help books on cognitive-behavioral therapy that will help a person suffering from emotional distress. CBT has certain strategies and a clear understanding. Each session has its own different plan or program. In each CBT session, asking questions is very important. The patient needs to pose all their concerns, so the psychologist has to pose the patient some concerns in order to be able to answer certain issues that the patient may not be able to articulate; there are moments that a patient might not be able to say what they actually think.

Through Cognitive-behavioral therapy, great approaches are learned, such as being able to change the way people think and behave. Positive thought is also a component of CBT and involves avoiding and stopping unconscious emotional thinking. The other important methods and tactics hinder one's style of talking and walking. An individual always wants comfort and relaxation because if comfortable and reassured, it becomes simpler for the treatment to settle into a person's brain. Often, the knowledge provided to patients is transmitted more quickly when a person is not overwhelmed or under strain.

Some sources provide useful details about Cognitive-behavioral therapy. Explanations and details are often provided for CBT and the therapies. Situations are presented in such a manner that families and associates of individuals with mental and behavioral issues have an understanding of the situation and how to fix it. There's even a history of CBT and other research regarding it. Additionally, posts and forums can be found on the Internet that provides valuable knowledge on this counseling. Some websites also provide CBT updates and blogs so people can connect with each other and exchange insights and feelings about it.

Cognitive-behavioral therapy (CBT) is a psychotherapy focused solely on cognitions, expectations, values, and attitudes that often seek to manipulate harmful feelings due to incorrect interpretation of incidents. The general approach is developed from the modification of behavior.

In terms of the results achieved, cognitive-behavioral therapy is considered among the most effective. The total number of clients attending the sessions is just 16. Certain therapy methods—such as psychoanalysis—can take years. What makes CBT briefer is its extremely instructive existence and the way that it includes homework.

How It Works

Cognitive-behavioral therapy can be helpful in making sense of overwhelming problems in the smaller parts that break them down. Thus, it is simpler to see how related they are to you. The pieces are usually a circumstance that may be troublesome, eventful, or challenging. This will imitate emotions, feelings, and acts.

Cautions

Cognitive-behavioral therapy also does not match all patients with this particular issue. Psychodynamic counseling can best support those who may not have a particular behavioral problem that they want to fix and whose motivations for counseling are to obtain insight into the experience. Patients also need to be prepared to take a very active part of the treatment process.

Cognitive-behavioral therapy with certain seriously depressed patients and people with cognitive impairments could be inadequate. Treatment for patients suffering from organic brain disease or traumatic brain injury depends on how well they function.

Treatment

CBT varies from other therapies as each session has a plan, rather than the participant simply thinking about something that comes to mind. The client meets with the therapist in the beginning to describe specific problems and to set goals they wish to work towards. Their problem may have some symptoms such as sleeping badly, being unable to socialize with friends, or having difficulty focusing on reading or working. Perhaps they may be life-threatening issues, such as a student being depressed at college, an underage boy experiencing difficulty coping, or a couple who is unhappily married. Then these issues and objectives become the basis for planning the content of the sessions and discussing how to handle them.

Cognitive-Behavioral Theories

Cognitive-behavioral therapy, or CBT, is a specific treatment that can help patients with multiple types of personality disorders such as social anxiety, psychotic depression, and post-traumatic stress syndrome. Cognitive-behavioral therapy is a modern and very goal-oriented form of therapy that many consider to be the most effective way to treat personality disorders today (even to move past the concept of medication).

The psychiatrist or therapist who presides over the sessions can continue the therapy by making the individual challenge their notions; for example, how can they be so confident that someone can still observe and assess them? The goal here is to attempt to modify the instinctual response of an individual to stimuli that cause stress. Throughout the "true world," people are given proves that their patterns of reasoning are not rational or simply "happening."

A significant part of CBT is the positive relaxation strategy. In this case, the doctor or therapist will force the patient to confront the things they fear, such as groups, speaking in public, or being the "center of attention." However, instead of forcing the patient to confront these fears haphazardly, the doctor will ensure that the confrontation takes place in a very structured and sensitive manner.

Another technique frequently employed in cognitive-behavioral therapy is "systematic desensitization." This entails the psychiatrist having the patient visualize the traumatic scenario that is taking place, simulating it in a manner, and then operating in a calm and regulated atmosphere despite the fears.

It is necessary to note that cognitive-behavioral counseling is not typically an easy procedure for clients to move through. The sessions are brief, particularly as compared to other therapy sessions. However, in order to replace dysfunctional behavior with adaptive coping mechanisms, clients must be helped to recognize when and why their mental processes deteriorate, and then some time is required.

Chapter 1: What Is Behavioral Therapy?

"Behavioral therapy," also known as "behavioral modification," is a theory-based learning approach to psychotherapy aimed at treating psychopathologies through techniques designed to strengthen desired behaviors and eliminate unwanted behaviors. Ancient philosophical traditions, such as stoicism, were the precursors of certain basic aspects of behavioral therapy. B.F. Skinner may have used the first occurrence of the term "behavioral therapy" in a research project in 1953. Nathan H. Azrin, Ogden Lindsley, Harry C. Solomon, Joseph Wolpe, and Hans Eysenck are other early pioneers in this type of therapy.

There are three distinct sources of behavioral therapy: South Africa (Wolpe's group), the United States (Skinner), and the United Kingdom (Rachman and Eysenck). In particular, Eysenck viewed behavioral issues as an interplay between the characteristics of environment, behavior, and personality. On the other hand, Skinner's group took more of an operational conditioning approach involving a functional approach to assessment and contingency management interventions (reward and punishment for positive and negative behavior (also known as the "token system) and behavioral activation.

Skinner became interested in individualizing programs to enhance people's learning—with and without disabilities; he worked with Fred S. Keller to develop programmed training.

Clinical success in treating aphasia rehabilitation was demonstrated by programmed instruction. Ogden Lindsley, a student of Skinner, is credited with forming a movement called "precision teaching," which developed a kind of graphics program that kept track of how much progress the clients made.

Many therapists began combining this therapy with Aaron Beck's cognitive therapy and Albert Ellis' cognitive-behavioral therapy in the second half of the 20th century. The cognitive component added to the therapy in some areas (especially when it came to treating social phobia), but the cognitive component did not add to the therapy in other areas. This has led to the pursuit of behavioral therapies of the third generation.

Third-generation behavioral therapies combine "operant" and "respondent" psychology's basic principles with functional analysis and a clinical formulation or case conceptualization of verbal behavior that incorporates more of the behavioral analyst's views. Research shows that in some cases, third-generation behavioral therapies are more effective than cognitive therapy, but more research is needed to make the evidence conclusive.

Behavioral therapy combines Ivan Pavlov's principles of classical conditioning with B.F. Skinner's principles of operant conditioning. There has been some confusion as to how these two conditions differ and how this has any common scientific basis for the different techniques. An online paper, "Reinforcing Behavioral Therapy," provides a response to this confusion. Operating conditioning has resulted in contingency management programs that have been quite effective even in adults with schizophrenia. Respondent conditioning has resulted in systematic desensitization and exposure and response prevention.

This has led many to believe that using behavioral therapy to treat depression, attention deficit hyperactivity disorder, and obsessive-compulsive disorder is as effective, if not more effective, than drug treatment. Habit reversal training is another successful form of therapy that has demonstrated great success. This has been shown to be highly effective in treating tics. The behavioral therapy characteristics include being empirical (data-driven), contextual (focusing on environment and context), functional (interested in the consequence or effect of a behavior), probabilistic (seeing the behavior as statistically predictable), monistic (treating the person as a unit and rejecting dualism between mind and body), and relational (analyzing bidirectional interactions).

Behavioral therapy has been developed from three different origins and has its roots in both operant conditioning and respondent conditioning. Third-generation Cognitive-behavioral therapies—widely used to great effect today—originated from behavioral therapy. These are just some of the reasons why it is so important in our world today to discover and develop behavioral therapy.

Mastering Emotional Regulation

The phenomenon of feeling controlled by other people within social settings is one of the worst problems we experience in life. With the implication that others are more in control than we are when we feel out of control, emotional regulation becomes a major challenge.

In these situations, our biggest mistake is to extend notions of control beyond what we can control. We delve into life areas that we don't care about. No wonder we're fighting because we've put ourselves in tenuous emotional positions.

It's just about disciplining ourselves to focus on what we can do and stop focusing on what we can't do.

"What can I do?" If we feel emotionally unhappy or just a little unhappy with a particular outcome, we can ask questions that us. We might be frustrated with the answer for a moment. Except to accept the situation as it is, we may not be able to do much. But there is an irony in control here.

It's not what the other person or people have done or are doing that matters, but it's what we've done and what we can do that makes the biggest difference in regulating our emotions.

We take too much responsibility and not enough responsibility for our own emotions and for the emotions of other people. No wonder we're confused about our impact. We need to focus again on what we can influence in order to emphasize personal control.

Whenever, within our own personal control, we accept the boundaries, emotional regulation never becomes easier. It also helps us see aspects of their brokenness and wholeness.

Their Brokenness and Our Wholeness

Too often, we see it the other way around—their wholeness and advantage and our brokenness and capacity shortages.

Seeing the fallibility of another person is a blessing to them as our grace forgives them for their character frailties. They're far from perfect, and so are we. They may do things to get us upset, but they have less control over their interactions with us than they want. And, seeing ourselves with a capacity for wholeness is nothing wrong.

If we're broken—and we're all broken—we also have wholeness aspects that should be celebrated.

Our personal control boundaries are our security with regard to our emotional regulation. The more we ask, "What can I do?" The more we strengthen our influence, our emotions are less like a roller coaster than a steady drive through the countryside is.

Self-acceptance

Self-acceptance is closely linked to "self-image." This is the picture you've built up about how good, successful, talented, or how unhappy and ugly you are. It is an image that has been built up throughout your lifetime, an image that is predominantly based on your successes and failures. Therefore, the first step in improving your self-acceptance is to improve your self-image and to do so, and you need to change the way you think about yourself.

Apart from improving your self-image, learning to accept yourself as you are now, with all your faults, is the most important thing to do. You can change some of your faults, deficiencies, and so on, and you should try to change them, but you have to accept them for now. Many people feel that they are too skinny, too fat, too short, not smart enough, or that their ears are too big, or that they don't have enough hair. If you have such shortcomings, it's important not to hate yourself—in many cases; they are things you were born with and can't do anything about. You don't have to be perfect, and no one is perfect. Say to yourself, "I'm not perfect, but so what? No one is." And "I'm going to make the most of what I have." Be your own. And the main reason is that your happiness and success depend on your self-acceptance to a large extent. Indeed, without it, it's hard to be really happy or successful. So stop trying to be perfect; look at yourself as you are. This doesn't mean you shouldn't make every effort to improve yourself—you should.

Also, your friends and associates have a great impact on your self-acceptance and self-esteem. You increase your self-acceptance and self-esteem when you believe they have a high opinion of you. On the other hand, if you think they have a low opinion about you, your acceptance of yourself usually falls apart. Therefore, making sure this doesn't happen is important. So, don't worry about what other people think; you're still wrong in most cases. Moreover, it is important to remember that, unless you let them, no one can make you feel bad about yourself. People often make remarks that are harmful to others without realizing it (and they do it on purpose, of course, sometimes). Don't be serious about taking offense. No one has anything to do with how you feel about yourself—unless you allow it. Learn to disregard them.

Sitting down and listing your accomplishments is one of the best ways to boost your self-acceptance and esteem. You might not think you've got a lot, but you might be surprised. Think about the goals you've achieved, the awards you've received, the years you've completed in school or university. Think of your accomplishments at work, your hobbies, etc. Read them when you're done. As you think about them, take pride in them.

Tips on Self-Acceptance Improvement

- Don't try to impress people.
- Focus on your life's positive things and appreciate them.
- Don't overlook your faults or weaknesses—accept them. Don't worry about them, but tell yourself that you are going to work to overcome anything that can be overcome.
- Choose a role model—someone you look up to and admire—and emulate their good points.
- Have objectives. It always makes you feel good to achieve goals.
- Don't apologize; don't constantly blame others, and don't complain.
- Learn from your errors.
- Revive your "best moments" (in your memory) occasionally. Remember your unique talents.
- Remember that everyone has things about themselves that they don't like. You're not on your own.

When you begin to worry about something you don't like about yourself, say to yourself, "Nobody's perfect. I'm not perfect, but no one else is perfect, and I'm a person. I thought I should put the needs of everyone else first. And this is not self-care?" Self-care is a concept that is often misunderstood. Taking care of yourself does not mean neglecting everyone else in your life. And BIG NEWS: Self-care has nothing to do with being selfish or a "bad person." Self-care is as essential to life as breathing. Before I go on, let me explain how I define self-care.

Why Else Would You Like to Take Good Care of Yourself?

Well, you can't give what you don't have if you're a caring person and responsible for caring for family members or others. If you're not healthy, energized, and balanced, how can you expect to attend to the health, energy, and happiness of someone else? If you give, give, and give, and never receive—from others or yourself—you're left with nothing, completely empty, without giving anything. I'm sure that many of you can relate to how your body, mind, and spirit feel that void.

There's a bucket in my favorite analogy. You have nothing left to give if your bucket is empty. The more your bucket is filled, the more it is necessary to give. Life is a constant process of filling and refilling—giving and receiving from your bucket. How are you going to refill the bucket? With self-care, self-love, self-nurturing... doing all the things that bring balance and joy to you. Self-care is the water supply that fills your bucket and lets you continue to give and love.

I don't suggest you take so much care of yourself that you forget others. That's not going to be good either. I suggest a good balance between self-care and care for others.

And one final thought... it is NOT self-care but self-preserving. It makes your life a LOT smoother. The happier you are, and the more balanced you are, the happier the others around you can be. To take good care of yourself is actually the most loving thing you can do for others.

Self-confidence

Self-confidence has to do with your ability to be confident. It's about how you feel you're doing the tasks that you're doing. And it's also how confident you are with your appearance. People who are self-confident are confident that they will be able to do well what is expected of them. However, it may not be something that will pervade all aspects of their lives. In some areas, most people are confident, but not confident in others. For example, they may be talented and confident in a specific sport, but they have little ability or confidence to speak to a group of people. It is also important to note that trust is not necessarily skill-related. Some people in a particular area with considerable ability do not feel confident. High confidence, but low self-esteem, is also possible. Many celebrities fall into this category; for example, many actors have a high level of trust in their ability to act but rely on drugs to see themselves through the day. People with low self-confidence usually seek other people's continued approval to feel good about themselves. They lose trust when they don't get it. They also often put themselves down, find it hard to accept compliments, and expect to fail.

So, how do you build confidence in yourself (assuming you don't have it)? Maybe it's not easy. Lack of trust is usually inspired by years of inferior feeling. Asking yourself what you really love to do is one of the best ways to start. It's much easier to do a task or job if you love it, and you'll feel more confident about doing it.

Sit down and list all the things you really enjoy doing, and make a list of your strengths while you're at it. Do they fit the things that you love to do? You'll have to think about how to bring them together if they don't. What are you going to need? More training? More education? Get that. Get it.

Next, focus on your strengths and forget about your shortcomings. This doesn't mean you ought to develop an unrealistic self-image; it means you ought to be honest with yourself. You should look at your skills and weaknesses carefully but always stress the positive.

We've all met people we admire, and often because they are so self-confident, that's the main reason we admire them. Trying to emulate them accurately is not a good idea, but you can learn how to form and incorporate some of their best traits into your personality. Tips to increase your self-confidence:

- Get rid of any negative thoughts as quickly as possible.
- Use self-talk and affirmations to encourage yourself,
- Achieve goals. It is important because achieving goals gives you considerable self-confidence.
- Be well-dressed and groomed.
- Be prepared for every task. By being well-prepared, you beat insecurity.
- Keep learning and studying, even if you think you know everything.

- Assess yourself (every so often, I undergo self-assessment).
- Smile as much as you can.
- Use visualization.

Therefore, let's try to explain why your mind is your greatest power. Everything in our universe is made up of vibrations of energy, as well as everything that appears stable in our physical world. These vibrating waves create even our thoughts, and they are the most dynamic and fluid substance in the cosmos as a whole.

Are you right now commanding your heart to beat? If not, what will it do? How does it affect you?

First, your thoughts are independent of, and yet interact with, the physical universe. What is amazing is that any thought in your conscious mind that is repeated over and over will then make an impression on your subconscious.

And once this mark makes it into your unconscious mind, it is then used as a tuning tool and starts to vibrate and attract the people, the circumstances, and the events that match the images you have inside. You have a real power to influence and direct the things that happen to you.

The Power to Influence

So, before you think about me in disbelief, let me make a point. Considering that you can do certain things, or are good enough, or are successful or wealthy, it must be difficult for you. Yet you think the opposite is true. So why would your mind be unable to believe one way but not the other?

One of the lovely things about the subconscious and its power is that it can't tell the difference between what's real and what you're thinking. So it means that anything you want can be programmed and printed into it.

And so, there have been experiments on this, where athletes predominantly imagine practicing for a month and then do the same as those who actually practiced. It resulted in their belief that they were good at improving their performance. Thus, imagining an action or a state of being on your mind over and over again gives your subconscious a profound impression.

Within the Soviet Union, the Powerful Source used it on their athletes. I know, I was one of them. But more importantly, it goes beyond sports and can be used for finance, relationships, career, and self-healing. When you work with mind power methods, there are no areas of your life that are impossible. It can be viewing, meditating, affirming, attracting, or creating new beliefs. You feel like you're taking control of your life.

Your thoughts are the most powerful source of food and abundance. But no one is teaching us how to think. We're learning to be positive or to do our best. Well, I'm sorry, but I'm sad. Positive thinking is essential, while mind power is at your disposal and is a powerful tool.

And anyone can easily understand the laws and methods. Once you realize that your thoughts affect your reality, it's a real awakening. You're ahead of millions of other people if you believe in mind power because it's still pretty much a recent theory. Only a small percentage of the world believes in it, and half are not practicing it on a daily basis or in the right way.

What is Mind Power?

Mind power is not only positive; it uses ways of impressing beliefs and images, not only on a conscious level—as it is with positive thinking—but on an unconscious level. Once you imagine and live the things you want, you attract those things to you again and again.

And there is no greater turning point in your life than to discover that you are the master of your destiny and that you have personal power. And all it takes to transform your life is perhaps fifteen minutes a day if you are ready to practice daily.

But remember that it can work against you in equal measure. The reason is that your thoughts can keep you in poverty, sickness, or failing to achieve your goals as well. Indeed, it's one of today's greatest tragedies. That's why most people don't come forward. Their mind power subconsciously attracts the wrong things into their lives. In truth, your thoughts create your reality.

Mind power and creativity inventions were often generated by creative people through ideas that came from nowhere, but always when they took time off. When you're too busy or working too hard, these things don't happen. You have to give yourself time for good quality and to honor yourself. So, you have to take days off when you don't work at all.

And when you let go of all, you give your creativity and intuition time to get in touch with the abundance of thoughts and mental power that you have at your disposal.

"Why do I always get my best ideas in the shower?" said Albert Einstein. So, it can make a difference even a little time away. Today, I am a big believer in just taking time off once in a while to reflect, evaluate, and evaluate things. If you attract things when you're frequently stressed or overworked, it's not going to do you any good.

You're a brilliant human-machine with mental power! What I realized is that all the successful people I know have made their fortune and have been successful in an area they loved. Think about it a second! Has anyone ever made a lot of money by doing something they don't enjoy doing?

I'm certainly not! Steve Jobs got into computers because he loved it, not because he wanted to be rich. That's also one of the success secrets. So find something you enjoy doing. Not only will you succeed in it, but you will have more fun doing it.

You win both ways. However, one of the maxims of mind power is that before you can get it, you must know what you want. And you have to make sure your goals are attached to a mission, purpose, or reason, or it's not going to last.

The First Step to Mind Power

Life's beautiful thing is that we can choose whatever goals we want. It's beautiful! Everyone has the right to live their existence differently when there is free will, and they have their definition of success.

As time goes by and you sometimes examine your goals, you may find that your motivations are not as accurate as you originally thought they were. So, you don't want to end up climbing the success ladder just to find out it's on the wrong wall. And that's why each of us has a midlife crisis in due course.

So, paying attention to the thoughts within your mind is the first step to mind power and changing your life. And then, accordingly, direct them. You have thousands of thoughts every day. So you have to become very aware of what you're thinking when you realize that your thoughts influence, affect, and help create your reality.

The Imprint of False Beliefs

It works with any area of your life, but let's take money as an example. Usually, what do you feel when you think about it? Is it hard to make that money? Do you think there's no good chance out there? Or do you never seem to have enough money?

And if these are the kinds of thoughts you think, then, unfortunately, you imprint that reality into your subconscious. You imprint into your subconscious with a consciousness of scarcity just by your day-to-day worrying and worrying about money. So once something is printed into your subconscious mind, it starts attracting the people, circumstances, and events that match the images you have on your mind.

So, you're blocking yourself from trying to get ahead financially in a never-ending experience of frustration. And how many hours a day you work, or the ideas you have, don't matter. If your money beliefs are limited, then you won't show out money.

Repetition is one of the most important aspects of making things happen. Your subconscious will accept any thought or belief you keep impressing. And the good news is that new prosperity beliefs can be reprogrammed and impressed.

So all you've got to do is repeat things over and over again and think it's true. And what's going to happen is that it's going to take an imprint every day, and it's going to change your money beliefs. Your mind power begins to attract better situations to you as you turn your points of view around.

Therefore, you have to be careful about the flow of thoughts within your mind. Take a look at those that match what you want. If you don't have the right thoughts, then by means of mind power techniques, you need to redirect your mind to a new place of belief. And develop a new prosperity awareness.

The Second Step to Mind Power

The first prosperity belief is that the universe is abundant. Everywhere you need to recognize prosperity and fill your mind with feeling, seeing, and being surrounded by wealth. Get a coffee and spend time in the most expensive place you know. Or look at and sit in your favorite car and imagine you own it.

Indeed, your mind power is not concerned with your gender, spiritual faith, or skin color. Many people in this world are becoming millionaires. They're not different from you at all. There's no reason why you can't succeed with prosperity beliefs, good ideas, initiative, and finding your calling.

So, you just have to find something about which you feel good. Even if you only choose to do what you love, there are still plenty of opportunities for you to operate and succeed. Another belief is that as Uncle G' always says, it is your duty and responsibility to succeed.

Honor Your Mind's Instinct

So you've got to honor what's calling you because it's not just what's going to make you successful; it's your contribution to the world as well. You've got to listen to that little voice telling you to move on. I don't say that it's going to be easy or that you're not going to get a couple of sleepless nights over it until you decide.

But if you honor the instinct of your mind power, it may be the best decision you can ever make. If you follow what you love, you may touch the lives of more people. You must follow your bliss, or what makes you jump for happiness. You can make a living doing something you don't like, but you're never going to succeed tremendously.

But the most fascinating, challenging, and exciting thing is that you can direct and influence your actions by choosing your thoughts. And you can create within you the energy vibrations that you need to attract realities.

You have to realize that you have at your disposal unlimited power. So spend 5 to 10 minutes a day contemplating, thinking, and affirming your own thoughts. After this little exercise, you may be excited for a few days. But there will be other times when that little voice comes in and says, "Who are you kidding? You don't have unlimited power." But every day, the critical factor here is to do it. Never miss a day, be it exciting or annoying. The power of the mind needs to be repeated. And you'll feel like an empowering conviction is taking over you somewhere along the 90-day period, as imprinting takes time. It may take longer sometimes.

So, this is what makes the difference between the power of positive thinking and mind power. The former is about "Think positive and positive things are going to happen to you." There's nothing wrong with that; I think that way rather than negatively. But beyond that, mind power is taking it a step.

Mind Power and Success

Mind power allows you to clearly define what you want. Then you add it through repetition and certain methods like affirmations, visualization, imprinting, creating new beliefs. So the subconscious starts picking it up.

So, give the right messages to yourself, and do some work on it every day as it doesn't happen magically. Make a list of 15 to 20 things that make you feel good and successful about who you are now and what you are. And the key here is 'Now.' However, you often think about your goals (things you're going to do or the changes you're going to make). Looking to the future is fine, but you want to create a success vibration now at the same time. Remember: More success is attracting.

Therefore, write down and make a list of things that make you feel like you're going to be successful right now. Then spend five minutes going over it every day, feeling successful about who and what you are now as you read it. It can be simple things like "I'm a great cook," "I'm a good friend," "I dress well," "I'm smart," and more. As a result, it's going to start creating a successful vibration now, so this frequency attracts other successes in the future. It's a pretty simple yet compelling technique. "My performance reviews are always positive. Why didn't I get a raise?" Express: Don't expect the other person to read your mind. Clearly express your opinions and emotions about the situation, "I think I deserve a raise." Assert: Assert your wishes. Ask specifically for what you want, "I want a raise. Are you going to give me that? Try not to tell others what they should do. Reinforce: Reward people who respond positively when you ask for something, express an opinion, or say no. You can reinforce people before they respond by listing the positive effects of getting what you are asking for. "I'll be more productive if I get a salary that reflects my value to this company."

Stay Mindful: Stay engaged. Don't mentally check out. Keep your focus on your goals and keep your position. Don't get distracted or put off by the other person.

Appearing Confident: It doesn't necessarily mean that you feel that way. Luckily, it works pretty well to act. Use a confident voice tone. You should be relaxed in your physical way. Give the right eye contact. Don't whisper or stammer on the floor. Act as if you're precious. Showing trust in any given situation is an appeal for judgment. There is a fine line between seeming too arrogant and too apologetic.

Negotiate: Be prepared not to get all you want. Be open to alternatives and offer something else to do or some other way to solve the problem. Turn the tables by asking them to suggest alternatives. Ask for their help, and be honest about it.

Learning to set limits, saying no, and asking what you want are important skills to build healthy self-esteem and interpersonal effectiveness. Dear Man of DBT divides it into discrete actions that increase the likelihood of a positive outcome.

Is Emotional Healing Important?

The prerequisite for physical healing is emotional healing. Research is increasingly showing that the mind's condition sets the tone for the body's condition. Negative years can make the body weak and sick. Some of our emotional turmoil is inevitable, of course. We all have emotional pain in our lives as a result of traumatic events.

Healing therapies can break the down cycle when we are trapped in pessimistic and discouraging thought cycles. We experience chronic hopelessness and depression if we hang out too long in these circles of unrest and unresolved conflict. This has a negative impact on the physical body in a way that is as real as a cigarette or staying up until 3 a.m. So how do we break the cycle and get emotional healing on the way?

A Two-Pronged Approach

Emotional healing comes in two ways. To recognize what is wrong, and then to shift your focus to happier things. It's important to face the reality of things that aren't right. Ignoring them will not work. But if you're just hanging out, you're not going to solve anything.

In massage and other healing therapies for the physical body, the best approach to healing is often to deal with it directly. This means a massage therapist will move into the area of dysfunction and release the body and restore circulation by dealing directly with the area of pain. Emotions must be treated in the same direct way. It's like getting a fluff and a buff spa massage when you really need deep tissue to deal with them by ignoring them or blurring them in your mind. The first step towards emotional healing is to recognize and face emotional trauma head-on. This can occur through counseling and psychotherapy, meditation, journaling, or other ways to focus on the places of pain.

And we have to move on; we don't have to hang out there. If we focus on life's thorns, we're never going to see the roses. They grow together, and it's our choice to concentrate most of the time. Good luck is a choice. This is where friendships are great therapies for healing. Within friendships, mutual giving and talking can do wonders for depression and anxiety, not only by facing it but above all by moving through it to a better place in your life. The stuff of friendship is joy and happiness. Those who nurture friendships have less anxiety, darkness, and desperation.

Other tools that enhance your journey to emotional healing, in addition to these two basic approaches, is the use of plant chemicals, such as herbal preparations and essential oils, which can make our journey to emotional health much easier. Psychotherapy with acupuncture, such as EFT, can be extremely helpful, and so can cranial electrical stimulation.

Now is the time to begin the journey to healing our emotions. Those who take responsibility for their lives come to emotional healing. If we don't, no one else is going to do it. So let's do our homework and plan in our lives today a few healing therapies.

Chapter 2: The History of Cognitive-Behavioral Therapy

Cognitive-behavioral therapy is an approach psychotherapists employ to influence the behaviors and emotions of a patient. The key to the approach is that it must be systematic in its procedure. It was widely used to manage a number of conditions, including eating disorders, drug misuse, anxiety, and behavioral disorders. It can be used in person or community counseling sessions, and the approach to self-help treatment may also be tailored.

Cognitive-behavioral therapy is a mixture of educational counseling and conventional behavioral therapy. They are combined into a treatment that focuses on eliminating the symptoms. The treatment's effectiveness can be specifically determined on the basis of its performance. The longer it is seen, the more popular it has been. It is now used as the number-one post-traumatic stress disorder treatment technique, as well as for obsessive-compulsive disorder, depression, and bulimia.

The earliest application of cognitive-behavioral therapy occurred from 1960–1970. It has been a gradual process of merging the behavioral and cognitive therapies' techniques. The behavioral treatment has been available since the 1920s, but it was not until the 1960s that cognitive counseling was adopted. The advantages of integrating it with behavioral counseling strategies were understood almost instantly. Ivan Pavlov was among the most famous of the pioneers of behavioral research with his dogs who salivated at the dinner bell ringing. Many field leaders included Clark Hull and John Watson.

Instead of relying on the treatment of the issue, such as Freud and the psychoanalysts, cognitive-behavioral counseling concentrated on removing the signs. The idea is that you eliminate the problem if you eliminate the symptoms. A more straightforward method has been shown to be more successful at moving to the issue at hand and allowing people to see more change.

Behavioral approaches cope more with more conventional conditions than non-traditional punitive therapy. The more evident and straightforward the signs were, the better it was for them to be identified and eliminated. Behavioral treatment— initially for more complex conditions such as addiction—was not as effective. The behavioral training methods have done this field well.

The two counseling methods were utilized side by side in many clinical contexts to evaluate and contrast the outcomes. It wasn't long before that the implications of integrating the two strategies were apparent as a way to take advantage of each one's strengths. David Barlow's research on overcoming panic disorder offered the first clear indication of the combination strategy's effectiveness.

In a concise term, cognitive-behavioral therapy is challenging to describe, as it encompasses such a vast variety of subjects and strategies. It is just a paragliding term for medical therapies that are uniquely adapted to a single patient's issues. So the problem dictates the treatment specifics, but some common themes and techniques do exist. Those involve the patient keeping a journal of significant activities and tracking their thoughts and actions connected with each case. This technique is also used as a framework for assessing and evaluating the patient's capacity to analyze the condition and establish an appropriate emotional reaction. It identifies negative emotions and behaviors, as well as the assessments and beliefs that lead to them. Then an attempt is taken to combat such convictions and judgments that prove that the underlying actions are false. Bad attitudes are removed, and a healthier approach for the individual to perceive and react to the problem is learned.

Much of the treatment often involves showing the individual strategies to divert or shift their attention from the disturbing or a circumstance that creates unpleasant behavior. Instead of the negative stimulus, they learn to focus on something else, avoiding the negative behavior that they would contribute to. Essentially the question is nipped in the bud. Mood-stabilizing drugs are also used or used in combination with methods for severe psychiatric conditions such as bipolar illness or schizophrenia. The medications offer the patient ample relaxing influence to enable them to analyze the condition and make a healthier decision, while before, they may not pause for critical thought.

With a number of conditions, Cognitive-behavioral therapy has been proved successful, but it is just a method, not a magic cure. Teaching people to consider circumstances and recognize the causes of their destructive habits requires time. When this phase is completed, it also requires a great deal of work to conquer their initial impulses and avoid making the same decisions again. They first know what they will be learning, and so they have to train before they do.

Understanding the Fundamentals of Cognitive-Behavior Therapy

Cognitive behavior therapy has been used to support patients with depression, anxieties, addictions, and all sorts of other psychosocial problems.

When a therapist uses cognitive-behavioral therapy, they help the person struggling to readjust his or her perception. It is known that thinking habits are associated with the individual's feelings and actions and the way a person may interpret or respond to other circumstances.

Cognitive-behavior therapy is a way to improve from a psychological point of view and identify the root causes of the problem and then alter or modify the thinking pattern that has contributed to the wrong behavior.

A practitioner utilizes cognitive-behavioral therapy to try to alter the patient's delusional and distorted thinking. This, in effect, will help the patient create behavioral changes and be able to adjust again. Thinking and feeling patterns play a vital role in human actions—which may be changed or adjusted.

Cognitive-behavioral therapy is often used to treat those recovering from opioid addictions, including heroin. In the strictest sense of the word, those who turn to drugs can be said to have a behavioral disorder and can gain from cognitive-behavioral therapy, including legitimate prescription drugs that are harmful as well as illegal drugs.

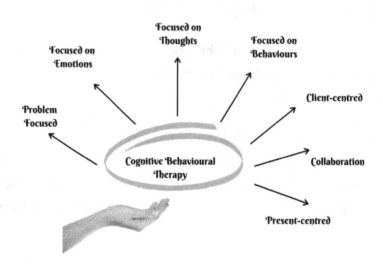

There are a growing number of people suffering from mental conditions, and while some claim the medical treatments may be adequate, studies appear to indicate successful results from cognitive-behavioral therapy. All depends, of course, on the client's ability to work with a trained therapist and to change inner thoughts and feelings.

The trained therapist also helps the patient understand past experiences and situations, analyze, and learn not to react in a distorted or irrational manner.

Cognitive-behavioral therapy has become a way of understanding the connection between human behavior and inner thoughts and perceptions. It has certainly led to some measurable progress. It has also made certain people make big life changes.

Whether you are a person with anxiety or depression, or some other form of the psychosocial disorder, take courage and locate a qualified cognitive-behavioral specialist. You can know how to create improvements in your life, so you can support yourself and others around you. Of course, making a change in your life may take you some time, but note that to do something meaningful you need dedication.

There are also several books written on this subject, which you may want to check out. You will also find lots of details when you go online that will help you know much more about cognitive-behavioral therapy.

The time that you might be investing would make a difference. The good news is that even if you sometimes feel overwhelmed and discouraged, there's help for you. In the form of workshops, there is also support that you can join to understand more about cognitive-behavioral therapy and how it can work. Taking the time to look through the available information could be your very first step towards recovery.

Characteristics of Cognitive-Behavior Therapy

Cognitive-behavioral therapy, or CBT, is a type of psychotherapy that is beneficial for a broad variety of difficulties in a person's life, such as depression, destructive behavior, anxiety, intimacy issues, unhealthy eating, ADHD, and bipolar disorder. CBT operates by modifying people's thinking, values (cognitive), and relationships (behavior).

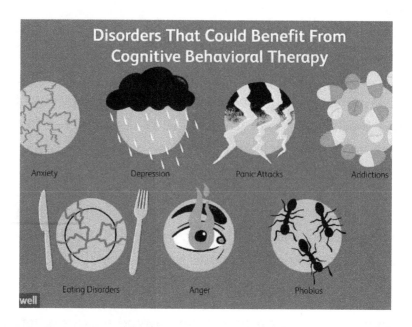

CBT encompasses a range of strategies from real relationships therapy (RLT), real-emotional-behavioral therapy (REBT), cognitive therapy (CT), rational behavioral therapy (RBT), acceptance and commitment therapy (ACT), mindfulness-based cognitive therapy (MBCT), dialectical-behavioral therapy (DBT), behavioral activation (BA), functional analytic psychotherapy (FAP), cognitive-behavioral assessment (CBT).

Given this variety, much of the cognitive-behavioral therapy is defined by:"

CBT Is Focused on a Method Which Triggers Emotional and Behavioral Responses to the Cognition

The way of thinking of the person creates their feelings and behaviors, rather than things like events, situations, and other people. Therefore, if we can change our thoughts, our feelings and behaviors will change accordingly.

CBT Is Constrained with Time

A course may be between 6 and 20 sessions. It will depend on several factors, such as the type of problem, the client's features, the therapist's experience, and so on, but in my opinion, changing the thinking habits of the client is the most important factor for ending CBT sessions.

Learning to Cope

CBT has more know-how to solve our problems. People do not learn a skill merely through reading and listening; learning and mastering any skill requires hard practice. Learning good thinking and dealing with problems properly is like learning swimming and surfing skills. When someone learns them, not only are they not afraid of oceans and waves but enjoy them.

CBT Is Goal-Oriented, Competitive and Organized

CBT is a collaborative effort between a psychiatrist and representatives of a client or group. The therapist's role is to listen, evaluate, educate, and inspire, and the client's task is to speak, learn, and practice about their problems." Sessions have a framework, and each session has its own individual purpose. The psychiatrist helps the individual accomplish desired objectives.

Do homework in CBT

Homework is known to be a critical component of CBT. It takes a long time to master CBT skills. The homework is designed and issued according to the expectations of the clients.

Person or Party Sittings

CBT should be achieved through one-to-one counseling or with a network of people. The advantages of cognitive-behavioral community counseling can include exposure to peer resources, improved cost efficiency, and enhanced encouragement.

The 3 Phases of Cognitive-Behavioral Therapy

In a nutshell, cognitive-behavioral therapy is a psychological method that is used as medical treatment based on its three primary areas.

Cognitive: It is the thought and of believing cycle.

Behavioral: It is what we do and how do we do it.

Emotional: It is happiness, harmony, energy, and power techniques.

People have frequently wondered whether this form of therapy would help. More importantly, scientific research has also shown that these methods can be more effective than drugs prescribed for depression, anxiety, and obsessive types. This is great news because medicines have known side effects, and CBT actually shows you how to handle the underlying problems with self-help methods and, in turn, help patients avoid relapses.

Your therapist will help you set realistic goals in the first step—the expectations that you have. This is done by taking a hard look at how you see things and helping you see things differently. Adjusting your thought cycle or your way of thinking, you're going to learn to put a spin on things in a positive way—things like If you've always assumed that only negative things are going to come your way, then they might. If you change your mindset, then you'll begin to anticipate better and safer results.

For example, your sessions have so many different angles to look from; just slow down, make rational thoughts that are also more automatic, focused, and determined. You can also expect to deal with anger, frustration, and overall, how you handle things.

This is how you customize all these changes to fit into your real-life situations in the next process. You will need a real understanding of these activities, so you can bring your newly learned interpersonal skills and strategies into the difficulties of your daily life. If you are suffering from social anxieties, you will need to feel a little more comfortable before getting in front of a group of people and delivering a speech.

You won't focus on the strength and power in the emotional therapy sessions; this will come naturally over time. You need to focus on relaxation. The brain needs to de-stress itself and be able to absorb calmness and quietness. This will eventually promote a healthier outlook on things as well as healing and happiness inside. There's a process here; allowing the peace and calm to expand slowly, you'll inadvertently let the anxieties, fear, and stress escape from nature.

Cognitive-behavioral therapy helps one understand that our emotions are responsible for our experiences and actions. There are certain causes that are not involved, such as individuals, events, and certain circumstances. This will allow us to benefit from understanding that we can change the way we look, think, and act even if our world may indicate otherwise.

Cognitive-Behavioral Therapy Skills to Help Yourself in Six Weeks

Cognitive-behavioral therapy may be the solution for many individuals who seek assistance managing stress, anxiety, OCD, or another mental, psychiatric, or behavioral issues. Cognitive-behavioral therapy (CBT) is ideal for someone who considers and focuses on their feelings! That's trickier, of course, than it sounds, but a good therapist can help you do that. Cognitive-behavioral therapy is particularly good for those who wish to be involved in improving themselves because it also gives you strategies and methods to handle the dilemma. Most people consider this a pleasant contrast to conventional therapy methods.

Unfortunately, there is often a lack of NHS (National Health Service) cognitive therapists (although this is changing), and you will still be placed on a waiting list. If you don't work due to your depression or other problems, or your ability to function in life activities is impaired, waiting is not an option.

Another alternative you need is to locate a private practitioner that provides CBT services. For example, there are the benefits to remember, and weeks of intensive treatment is out of the picture for certain individuals. CBT is a time-limited therapy (usually the maximum amount of sessions needed is from 5–15), so a successful psychiatrist should negotiate with you about the number of sessions that you are going to take to function within that setting. This is reviewed regularly throughout the therapy process and may require more or fewer sessions, depending on your progress.

I believe that if you're motivated to help yourself (the will needs to be there; your therapist will help you motivate yourself if you're depressed), and if you feel you can help yourself if you only have the tools and you're willing to practice techniques between sessions, then you can use cognitive-behavioral therapy to start your recovery journey in just six hours.

In reality, I notice that clients who decide to operate within a time frame of six months often understand the simple CBT strategies and how to implement them; they are inspired by the idea that therapy finishes. Sometimes these clients can make the best of counseling appointments taking an active interest and working with us (therapists).

If you find this plan will fit for you, then you should be recommended to a private practitioner in the field that you want to continue with and operate within a 6-month time frame. If you have a long-standing and more complex problem, you may need more long-term input so your therapist can advise you on this.

Here is an example of what cognitive-behavioral therapy can teach you in six weeks:

Week 1: Application to the CBT system and how the issue applies to it. Recognition of the connection between perceptions, emotions, and actions. Learning to keep the thoughts in order. How to recognize "soft thought."

Week 2: Studying the dictionary of thoughts and learning how to question your own unhelpful thoughts. Analyzing the facts for and against your cognitions and recognizing mistakes in the transmission of knowledge. Learning to substitute skewed definitions with fair, adaptive definitions.

Week 3: Identification of basic foundation (schema) values. Beginning to find strategies to counter old divisive values and restructure new resilient principles. Designing hypotheses on your own behavior.

Week 4–6: Cognitive and behavioral experiments and activities as the therapist and client decide to target specific difficulties for the client. For example, learning anxiety management and mindfulness techniques, graded avoidance awareness, activity scheduling, and activity logs to tackle inactivity and poor motivation. Exercises in self-esteem and the scheduling of pleasurable low-mood activities.

A CBT therapist will also usually expect the client to supplement with homework activities and sometimes reading what is learned during the sessions. Clients are usually required to maintain a six-week thought diary, and this is reviewed at each session along with other homework.

What Constitutes Cognitive-Behavioral Therapy?

Cognitive-behavioral therapy is a psychotherapeutic approach aimed at teaching a person new skills on how to solve problems relating to dysfunctional emotions, behaviors, and cognitions through a goal-oriented, systematic approach. In several cases, this term is used for differentiating behavioral counseling, cognitive treatment, and counseling focused on both clinical and cognitive interventions. There is empirical evidence that cognitive-behavioral therapy is quite effective in treating multiple conditions like temperament, fear, attitude, drinking, abuse of substances, and psychotic disorders. Treatment is often individualized, as specific psychological orders are treated with specific, brief, direct, time-limited, and technique-driven treatments. Cognitive-behavioral therapy can be used in groups as well as with individuals. The techniques are also frequently adapted for self-help sessions. Whether he/she is more cognitive-oriented, more behavioral-oriented, or a combination of both, depends on the individual clinician or researcher, as all three methods are used today. Emotional behavioral treatment was developed out of a mixture of cognitive and physical therapies. These two treatments have many variations. However, there is common ground to concentrate on the "here and now" and symptom relief.

Evaluating cognitive-behavioral therapy has led many to believe that psychodynamic treatments and other methods are more effective than this. The UK advocates the use of cognitive-behavioral therapy over other methods for many mental health problems, including post-traumatic stress disorder, obsessive-compulsive disorder, bulimia nervosa, clinical depression, and chronic fatigue syndrome (myalgia encephalomyelitis) of the neurological condition. The precursors of cognitive-behavioral therapy are rooted in different ancient philosophical traditions, notably stoicism. The modern roots of CBT can be traced back to the development of behavioral therapy in the 1920s, cognitive therapy development in the 1960s, and subsequent merging of the two therapies. In 1924, Mary Cover Jones published the first therapeutic approaches to behavior, and her work dealt with the unlearning of fears in children.

The early approaches to behavior worked well with many of the neurotic disorders but not so much with depression. The "cognitive revolution" also caused behavioral therapy to lose popularity, which eventually led to the founding of cognitive therapy by Aaron T. Beck in the 1960s. Arnold A. Lazarus created the first cognitive-behavioral therapy method during the time frame from the late 1950s through the 1970s. Cognitive and behavioral treatments were merged throughout the 1980s and 1990s by research conducted by David M. Clark in the UK and David H. Barlow in the United States.

The following methods include integrated behavioral counseling: Systematic rehabilitation, logical social behavior treatment, and multimodal counseling. One of the greatest problems is to describe just what cognitive-behavioral therapy is. The specific therapeutic techniques vary among different CBT approaches depending on what kind of problem issues are being addressed, but the techniques usually centered around the following:

- Maintaining a journal documenting significant incidents and their emotions, opinions, and habits.
- Questioning of contradictory and unhelpful cognitions, perceptions, conclusions, and values.
- Activities that could have been prevented slowly meet.
- Trying out new ways to behave and react.

In addition, distraction techniques, mindfulness, and relaxation are also commonly used in cognitive-behavioral therapy. Medications to improve the mood are sometimes paired with treatments that manage disorders such as bipolar disorder. The NICE guidelines within the British NHS accept the use of Cognitive-behavioral therapy in conjunction with medication and therapy in treating schizophrenia. Cognitive-behavioral therapy typically requires time to integrate it successfully into people's lives. For them, it usually takes concerted effort to replace a cognitive-affective-behavioral pathological mechanism or pattern with a more rational and efficient one, even when they know when and where their mental processes go wrong. In many different situations, cognitive-behavioral therapy is implemented including the following conditions:

- Fear disorders (obsessive-compulsive disorder, social phobia or social apprehension, common anxiety disorder)

- Mood disturbances (clinical depression, a severe depressive illness, psychiatry signs)
- Insomnia (including providing better potency than Zopiclone)
- Severe mental disorders (severe depression, schizophrenia, bipolar disorder)
- Children and teens (major depressive disorder, anxiety disorders, trauma, and symptoms of post-traumatic stress disorder)
- Stuttering (helping them conquer fear, avoidance habits, and pessimistic self-thinking)

Cognitive-behavioral therapy involves teaching a person new skills through a goal-oriented, systematic approach to overcome dysfunctional emotions, behaviors, and cognitions. Empirical research suggests that cognitive-behavioral counseling is successful in the management of multiple disorders, including obsessive-compulsive disorder, common anxiety illness, severe depressive disorder, ADHD, paranoia, and self-negative thinking. With the vast amount of success demonstrated by using this therapy, it is one of today's most important tools that researchers and therapists need to treat mental disorders.

How Does CBT Differ from Other Types of Counseling?

The Evidence

CBT's most significant distinguishing feature is the evidence to back it up. The National Institute of Clinical Excellence (NICE the federal agency responsible for delivering public health service guidelines on the advancement of healthy well-being and the avoidance and diagnosis of ill health) advises it as the medication of choice for a variety of mental health issues like panic, depression, obsessive-compulsive disorder, post-traumatic stress disorder, and eating disorders. The effects of CBT have been demonstrated time and time again in randomized control studies (the most rigorous way to determine whether a cause-effect relationship exists between treatment and outcome), and a wealth of published research studies support its effectiveness (e.g., Cochrane Review of a group of more than 10,000 volunteers in more than 90 countries testing the effects of health care interventions). CBT is the first psychotherapeutic method with such a strong base of facts over a variety of behavioral well-being problems.

A Short Term Medication

CBT is also viewed as a 'short-term treatment,' and while it is definitely time-limited relative to other forms of 'talking therapy,' it is necessary to refute the misconception that it is a fast cure. CBT is used to address problems that conflict with an individual's ability to work in one or more aspects of their lives. These issues are real, significant, and often long-standing, so it is reasonable that a certain amount of time and energy will be needed to solve such problems. An issue that is simple and easy-to-fix does not require a highly qualified and skilled counseling course. The number of CBT sessions a person needs depends on the severity and chronicity of the symptoms, but between 15–20 sessions is a minimum average. Many other psychotherapeutic services will extend for years (e.g., psychodynamic psychotherapy). The features that allow CBT to be a 'short-term' treatment are also key in distinguishing it from other psychotherapeutic strategies.

Issue-Based and Goal-Driven

CBT is focused on solving specific issues. During the initial assessment (first 1–3 sessions), the therapist will develop a problem formulation that will allow both therapist and patient to understand how the problem has developed and why it has not been resolved (up to this point). This definition is also used to direct treatment towards concrete targets (identified collaboratively by the therapist and patient), which, when achieved, would mean the cure of the question posed. The original issue design should be checked and revised during the procedure to provide new details that could come to light, and the therapy will be monitored at periodic intervals to ensure progress towards the target objectives is achieved. This shared understanding of the problem and a clearly defined end goal ensure treatment is as efficient and effective as possible.

Becoming Your Own Therapist

CBT's ultimate goal is to have the patient become his own therapist. The therapist is set up as the 'expert' in some types of counseling, who imparts knowledge of a seemingly inaccessible nature that can leave the patient feeling dependent on the therapist and undermine their confidence in their own ability to solve problems. CBT therapists and counselors collaborate together to allow people to develop a range of skills (practical and psychological) that can be combined with their own experience so that they can potentially overcome not only present challenges individually but also resolve potential issues without the need for more therapy. This ensures that only one course of therapy is typically expected, and thereby, the probability that feedback of 'longer-term' would be requested. This aim is illustrated in the following analogy:

"An oyster creates a pearl from a grain of sand. A Sand grain is an irritant to the oyster. In reaction to the pain, the oyster produces a smooth defensive layer that encloses the sand and offers relaxation.

"An irritant is the seed for something good for an oyster. Likewise, CBT counseling will help you grow more positive about your present frustration. The skills learned... can make you feel happier and can continue to have meaning in your existence even after the initial issues are gone."—Padesky & Greenberger 1995

A 'Here and Now' Therapy

However, it is important to be clear about what this means since this term is often misunderstood and used to imply that CBT is not suitable for solving complex problems. In the initial step of CBT, the emphasis is on alleviating the symptoms actually encountered by the patients (e.g., heart problems, depressed mood) by resolving the causes that prevent them. This is required not simply to provide the patient with relaxation, but if necessary (i.e., with severe/long-standing problems) to unlock the patient's potential to concentrate on investigating and addressing the issues that first led to the issue. In this second step of therapy (often perceived to be the realm of long-term psychotherapeutic approaches), an expanded (but less popular) variant of CBT (Schema-Based CBT) is utilized and has been deliberately designed to insure that changes 'here and now' are maintained and to defend against potential recurrences. Although this second step increases the duration of therapy—since it proceeds to incorporate the above-mentioned function—it provides a much more time-efficient approach to fix long-standing concerns than certain forms of counseling commonly used to resolve these issues.

The British CBT & Counseling Service is an organization of clinical psychology and counseling psychologists (MSc) (Richmond, Kingston, Nottingham) specializing in cognitive-behavioral therapy (CBT) for both adults and children with a range of problems including anxiety, depression, relationship problems, bereavement, eating disorders (including anorexia nervosa and bulimia nervosa), obsessive disease. We deliver CBT counseling face-to-face, mobile, marriage counseling, and internet consultation.

Chapter 3: Cognitive-Behavioral therapy - The Basics

Cognitive-behavioral therapy is a form of psychotherapy that stresses the important role that thinking plays in how we feel and what we do.

There is no cognitive-behavioral treatment as a separate clinical strategy. The term "Cognitive-behavioral therapy (CBT)," for a classification of therapies with similarities, is a very general term. Cognitive-behavioral counseling includes many forms, including moral-emotional-behavioral therapy, objective-behavioral therapy, good life therapy, cognitive psychology, and dialectic-behavioral therapy.

Most cognitive-behavioral therapies, however, have the following characteristics:

CBT is based on a Cognitive-Emotional Response Model

Cognitive-behavioral treatment is focused around the premise that our emotions (not external things), including objects, circumstances, and incidents, affect our feelings and actions." The benefit of this fact is that even if the situation doesn't change, we can change the way we think, feel to then 'act better.

CBT is Time-Limited and Briefer

In terms of the results obtained, Cognitive-behavioral therapy is considered among the most rapid. The average number of clients receiving sessions (over all types of CBT problems and approaches) is only 16. Other forms of treatment can take years— such as psychoanalysis. What makes CBT briefer is its extremely instructive nature and the fact that it uses homework tasks. CBT is time-limited in that at the very beginning of the therapy process; we help clients understand that there will be a point when the formal therapy is to end. The cessation of formal therapy is a judgment of the therapist and the client. CBT is, therefore, not an open-ended, interminable process.

A sound Therapeutic Relationship

For effective therapy, a sound therapeutic relationship is necessary but not the emphasis. Some forms of therapy assume that the main reason people get better in therapy is that the therapist and the client have a positive relationship. Cognitive-behavioral therapists think a healthy and trustworthy friendship is necessary but not enough. CBT practitioners claim the people are improving as they are studying how to behave differently and building on the experience. CBT practitioners also concentrate on developing appropriate self-control techniques.

CBT Is a Collaborative Effort Between Patient and Therapist

Cognitive-behavioral therapists seek to learn from life what their clients want (their goals) and then assist their clients in achieving those goals. The therapist's role is to listen, teach, and encourage, whereas the client's role is to express concerns, learn, and implement that learning.

CBT Has a Stoic Theory As Its Base

Not all CBT methods include stoicism. Stoicism is reinforced by logical-emotional-behavioral therapy, moral-behavioral therapy, and ethical living care. Cognitive therapy for Beck is not focused on stoicism. Cognitive-behavioral therapy doesn't dictate how people should feel. However, people seeking treatment often don't want to feel the way they do. The methods that stress stoicism demonstrates the advantages of feeling calm while faced with unwanted situations, at worst. They always underline the fact that we are getting our unwanted situations whether we are angry about them or not. If we're frustrated about our issues, we're having two problems—the issue and our frustration over it. Most people want the fewest possible number of problems. And as we begin to consider a personal dilemma more confidently, we not only feel happier but also place ourselves in a stronger position to use our intellect, experience, time, and abilities to solve the issue.

CBT Employs the Socratic Method

Cognitive-behavioral therapists are looking to gain a very good understanding of their clients' concerns. That is why they ask questions often. We always encourage clients to pose questions such as, "Why do I really realize what people are laughing at me?" "Do they laugh at something else?"

CBT Is Structured and Is a Guideline

For each course, the cognitive-behavioral practitioners have a specific agenda. During each session, specific techniques/concepts will be taught. CBT focuses on the clients' priorities. They don't tell our clients what their objectives will be or accept what they will. We are directives in the sense that we are demonstrating to our clients how to think and behave in appropriate ways to get what they want. CBT therapists, therefore, don't tell their clients what to do; rather, they teach their clients how to do it.

The CBT Is Focused Upon a Concept of Instruction

CBT is focused on the premise that certain cognitive and behavioral responses are learned. The goal of the therapy is, therefore, to help clients unlearn their unwanted reactions and learn new ways to react. But CBT has little to do with just speaking. People can talk to anyone, "just talk." CBT's educational voice has an added benefit—it leads to long-term success. Once people understand how they do better and why they do well, they know what to do to keep doing well.

The Inductive Method Relies on CBT Theory and Techniques

A central aspect of rational thinking is that it's fact-based. We often get upset about things when, in fact, the situation is not the way we think it is. If we knew that, we wouldn't be wasting our time getting upset. The inductive method, thus, encourages us to look at our ideas as theories or assumptions which can be challenged and evaluated. If we find our hypotheses wrong (because we have new information), then we can change our thinking to be in line with the actual situation.

Homework Is a Hallmark of CBT

If you spent only one hour per week studying, then, when you tried to learn your multiplication tables, you might still wonder what 5x5 equals. You've very probably spent a lot of time studying your multiplication tables at home, perhaps with flashcards. The same is true for psychotherapy. Goal achievement (if attained) could take a very long time. Only if all an individual had to care about the strategies and subjects learned was one hour a week. This is why CBT practitioners are giving reading tasks and motivating their clients to exercise acquired strategies.

The Value of Cognitive Therapy

We have to face quite a few specific kinds of problems and events in life. Any of those might be nice; others might not be so fun. But how we live life and whether we love it or loathe it is a feature of the kind of outlook we have as well as the emotional strength we can muster up. There are some individuals who are always optimistic and positive, allowing themselves with power and equanimity to deal with all circumstances. There are others on the other end of the scale that are very timid and also negatively predisposed, which makes them quite scared, scared, and also quite intimidated by each and everything.

While in some other cases, some people are cynical by nature, people also go through traumatic experiences that change their lives forever. For example, children who experience a murder or potentially a terrorist attack could become mentally marred for life and be given panic and anxiety attacks. To the point that they are perennially miserable or perhaps grouchy and grumpy and angry all the time, certain others get harried and hassled too. In any case, these are all examples of behaviorally dysfunctional actions and lifestyles that need to be treated through cognitive-behavioral therapy, also known as CBT.

CBT is a therapy through which professional clinicians and psychologists work alongside people to try to help them find the reason why they are behaving in a particular way with themselves. Thoughts provide a ride to emotions and spawning behavior and render it important to tackle thoughts and also properly analyze them so that the root cause of the problem can be identified and resolved. The key strategy is to substitute depressive feelings with constructive and optimistic ones for the individual to have a positive nature. Only in this way can one once again become healthy and happy.

We do not take for granted that CBT is a very easy technique. Of course, it needs a lot of meticulous and long-drawn psychoanalysis methods as well as psychiatric therapy for those old memories and deteriorating or wounded emotions to be allowed to disappear into the past. This will help bring happiness to the forefront and help a person make rational and healthy choices too. After all, it is crucial to ensure that life is lived to the fullest is crucial.

Cognitive-Behavioral Therapy and the Power of Thoughts

Evidence on the efficacy of Cognitive-behavioral therapy (CBT) in the management of multiple mental health conditions, including fear, depression, and addiction, is comprehensive. CBT puts emphasis on the power of thinking and believing. CBT includes several structures that have to understand and explore. I'll focus on three basic ones: Core beliefs, underlying assumptions, and automatic thinking.

What is the main conviction? It's how we come to look at ourselves and for potential. It is our unique pair of the lens through which we see the world. Such convictions are responsible for inducing unconscious reasoning. Unconscious thinking is a feeling that automatically occurs. It is our internal experiences that some circumstances cause. Maintaining control of unconscious thinking is a smart thing. Also, we don't really consider any of the derogatory self-talk we do every day. Journaling may be useful to slow, analyze, and evaluate what's going on in our heads. Questions to ask yourself while newspapering: "Which emotion has been experienced? Which thought has caused this negative emotion? What has occurred during that period?"

Identifying these unconscious thoughts and then looking further will reveal the ideas and fundamental values behind them. It is like peeling layers off an onion to reveal the central conviction. Automatic thoughts are the first few layers to elaborate on this metaphor, underlying assumptions form the middle layers, and ultimately core beliefs are the onion core. In cognitive-behavioral therapy, the uncovering of core beliefs is called the "downward arrow technique." Through this process, I find that my clients gain a great deal of self-awareness.

"I'm not good enough, or I'm not lovable," could be a core belief. So, how does an individual come to believe this? The underlying assumption determines the conviction or 'schema.' Usually, an underlying assumption is in the context of an "if... then" sentence. Usually, the individual does not question them, and they are taken as facts rather than as subjective opinions.

Here is an example of an assumption that underlies:

"If everyone likes me, then that means I'm a worthy person, and I will feel good about myself."

But not everybody can love the person all the time! This fundamental warped perception will set the person up in such a way that he or she continues to feel like a failure. By way of example, a critic's bad review could be translated as "I'm not approved, so that must imply something is wrong with me... I mustn't be a worthy individual."

Someone who is distressed will ignore or dismiss the good factors or events of their life and will focus on only the troubling 'data' that reinforces the central conviction (i.e., "being inadequate"). And it can take many positive thoughts or affirmations to debunk a deeply rooted negative belief repeated on a daily basis.

As you might think, dealing with these pessimistic core beliefs, or schemes (such as "I'm not lovable"), is complicated. Some turn from this negative state of mind to drugs from time to time for a brief escape. And for some, this ill-adapted method of coping will transform into a full-blown addiction. Core values can affect day-to-day activities and essential life decisions. I believe a vital aspect of the recovery process is learning to identify negative core beliefs and then challenge the assumptions that hold them.

The Effectiveness of Cognitive-Behavioral Therapy

Cognitive-behavioral therapy (CBT) is an approach that addresses behavioral, dysfunctional emotions and cognitive processes based on a combination of core behavioral principles and cognitive techniques. CBT is used by problem-focused and action-oriented approach practitioners to support people coping with common conditions such as fear, stress, and often more complicated psychological disorders.

Cognitive-behavioral therapy refers to a number of structured psychotherapy methods centering on the thoughts behind the problems of a patient. A survey of nearly 2,300 psychologists in the U.S. found that about 70 percent use CBT in combination with other therapies to treat depression and fear. CBT is also a predominant psychotherapy paradigm that is taught in graduate psychology programs.

How Does Cognitive Therapy Work?

Cognitive-behavioral therapy is based on the idea that human beings are somewhat irrational and make many illogical mistakes whenever they assess the risks and benefits of their thoughts and actions from different situations and courses. It can relate to feelings that are out of balance, such as rage and depression. But, CBT is also used to address a number of other nuanced problems, including post-traumatic stress disorder (PTSD), OCD, drug misuse, ADHD, eating disorders, bipolar disorder, and other illnesses.

For them to be successful, cognitive-behavioral clinicians will have a strong interaction with their clients, such as positive listening skills and a good personality fit. This is because the patient and therapist are working together to discuss the issues at hand and the reasons for the patient's thoughts and actions toward those issues. The end aim is to alter ways of thinking so that the individual feels less consistently unpleasant mental conditions.

The "Global Coalition for Behavioral Well-being," in favor of CBT, has outstanding research evidence promoting its application in the therapeutic diagnosis of mental illness, which has gained broad acceptance among both clinicians and patients alike. Increasing numbers of psychologists, psychiatrists, social workers, and psychiatric nurses are getting CBT training.

Research on CBT's effectiveness has been found to be effective against a wide range of disorders. Those experiments are well-controlled: the data is properly reviewed, and the findings speak for themselves. For starters, CBT has been shown to have substantial advantages when managing bipolar depression, culminating in fewer treatment days, reduced suicide rates, and decreased levels of para-suicidal or self-injurious behavior.

Precautions to be Taken Before Beginning Relational Cognitive Therapy

Psychiatrists, behavioral psychologists, social workers, and other mental health professionals undergo years of training and education, but without that solid training experience, it is possible to practice counseling. Before settling for a CBT specialist, other items to study include educational background and qualifications, along with any professional associations to which they belong, such as the "Organization for Behavioral and Cognitive Therapies," where most top practitioners are participants.

Review their history, schooling, credential, and license before seeing and making your first appointment. The general term psychotherapist is often used. Make sure the therapist you choose meets the requirements of state certification and licensing for their particular discipline. The key is finding a qualified therapist who can match your needs and also for the type of therapy. CBT is more effective in most situations when paired with various therapies, such as taking medicine. So you might also need a psychiatrist to prescribe medications besides your therapist.

The cost is one more thing to consider. When you have health care, find out what pays for all the treatment services it provides. Some health plans cover just a certain number of therapy sessions a year. Some may not even be covered. So, make sure to negotiate the costs and payment plans with the psychiatrist before the first meeting.

Think of what issues you're experiencing require care when you first assign. Although you should still work some of that out with your psychiatrist, a clearer understanding of your issues will serve as a beginning point in advance. Check again for their qualifications and experience, especially with your questions. Some therapists may not meet the qualifications requisite. If the first time around you don't find the right one, don't give up. Do the research, and locate a reliable cognitive-behavioral therapist.

Emotional Habits and CBT

It is commonly said that human beings are creatures of habit.

Typically, this definition is used in relation to our behavior, though in recent years, we have noticed that the way we think is also commonplace. Since we all realize that how we think has a great deal to do with how we act, a good question to ask is, what are my emotional habits?

What Are the Emotional Habits?

Emotional habits do have two dimensions:

How we generally feel as we go about the task of living our lives day after day.

If we react emotionally (again and again) to particular situations/events occurring in our lives.

The thoughts and emotions cannot be separated; they exist in unison during almost every moment of life. To be a person, in other terms, is to be in a state of continuous thinking and feeling—and the implicit complexities of that continuing subjective experience are partly normal.

Anxiety behaviors, depression, anger, irritability, helplessness, frustration, envy, fear, and worried about what others think of us, anxiety, and so on.

When we feel constantly nervous about what our future holds or frustrated and insecure about how our lives compete with others, it can be said that we have become used to repeating patterns.

This is not to condemn oneself or minimize the impact of real-life events and situations. The point is to put us in the driver's seat and suggest that if we've been used to these habits, then we can reaccustom ourselves to them and to other healthier trends.

Beware of the Oversimplification of CBT (Cognitive-Behavioral Therapy)

CBT is of enormous benefit to people all over the world and for the field of mental health in general. However, the oversimplified assertion that you can alter your mindset and change your life (as it happens in media sound-bites) can misinterpret the true essence and meaning of CBT and the related psychotherapy methods it has encouraged.

Why?

And it means that it's quick and convenient to adjust your outlook (like adjusting your shampoo or something). This may even bring us to the mistaken assumption that the job is done because you're 'changing your mind.' That cannot be any further from the facts. To become agents of change in regard to our own ways of thinking and feeling is analogous to learning and mastering a musical instrument, which I will talk about in a minute.

First, another argument regarding the possibility of oversimplifying CBT. Let us look at this idea, which is often heard:

It is not what happens to us that matters the most, but how we react to what happens to us.

I couldn't be more decided. However, it is crucial that we go a move forward and explain that our INITIAL response/reaction to 'stuff' is not nearly as crucial as how we reply overtime—over the course of the hour, day, week, month, and year.

We might blow up, shut down, stress out, diminish, take no notice, fall down, have a heart attack, etc. Okay, great, so what are we doing THEN? And after that, THEN... what do we do? And so forth.

My point is that what matters most is not the discreet moments but the ongoing (and always imperfect) process of striving for a good living. It is important to do that because we question ourselves:

Is my fundamental orientation to a life centered on constantly seeking to learn and grow from the challenges and complexities of life?

Am I leading a more emotional existence of accusing someone, avoiding responsibility, and constantly whining that things are not the way I would like them to be?

Changing thinking and emotional patterns is like learning to play the guitar.

It's lifelong learning to become someone who can play the guitar (which I do), and I think most would agree that it's ideally pursued as a love job. The same is true, in my view, for learning to change our thinking and emotional habits.

Yes, in our efforts to learn any musical instrument, there are 'techniques' that we employ. The most critical part of studying how to play an instrument, though, is NOT the strategies or methods, nor is it the teaching system or even the teacher's standard. What counts most is the degree of enthusiasm and commitment that the student brings to the project, along with the amount of artistic practice and success they put in overtime.

The Ethos of Continuous Learning and Development

We have also been born in a society riddled with social signals encouraging instant gratification and an attitude of rapid obsession. So it's no surprise we've built an over-reliance on shortcuts, suggestions, and the "newest cutting edge" strategies.

In reality, they don't offer the goods; what really succeeds in doing something meaningful is to apply the fundamentals over and over again while actively drawing on the gradual experience and ability increases.

In the school of life, the mentality of "pulling all-nighters" and "cramming" for exams will not represent us well; what truly matters in this realm is a sincere and consistent dedication to ideals and activities that best suit us and others.

Cognitive-Behavioral Therapy for Anxiety—Does It Work?

Understanding Your Anxiety

Disproportionate responses of worry and tension do characterize anxiety.

Anxiety is a natural feeling characterized by emotions from worrying thought, as well as physical changes such as increased tension and blood pressure.

Understanding the differences between normal emotions, anxiety, and anxiety illness (which needs urgent medical attention) can assist someone in identifying and managing the disorder.

Anxiety is a natural and usually healthy feeling. However, when someone regularly experiences disproportionate amounts of anxiety, this might become a medical disorder.

Anxiety illness forms a group of mental health diagnoses that cause excessive worry, fear, nervousness, and apprehension.

When Anxiety Requires Treatment

While anxiety might lead to distress, it is not often a medical condition.

When a person experiences potential worrying or harmful feelings, triggers of anxiety are not just normal but essential for survival.

Since evolution, the procedure of incoming danger and predators set off triggers in the body and has led to evasive or attack response. These triggers become noticeable in the form of a raised heartbeat, increased sensitivity, and profuse sweating.

The danger leads to a rush release of adrenalin, a chemical messenger in the mind, which in turn stimulates these anxious reactions.

For most people, running from imminent harm is a less urgent concern than it would have been for early beings. Anxieties now operate around health, work, family life, money, and other important matters that require a person's close attention without essential requiring a "flight-or-fight" response.

The feeling of being nervous before a crucial life situation or in a challenging event is a natural reaction of the natural flight or fight response. It is still important for survival.

Anxiety Disorders

The severity period of an anxious emotion can disproportionate the original stressor or trigger. Physical signs or symptoms, such as nausea and increased blood pressure, may be seen. These reactions move above the normal, natural anxiety into an anxiety disorder.

A person with an anxiety disorder has recurring intrusive concerns or thoughts. Once anxiety is in a disordered state, it can affect your daily routine.

Symptoms of Anxiety Disorder

Different diagnoses constitute anxiety disorder, and the symptoms of the generalized disorder will usually include the following:

- Difficulties in concentrating
- Difficulties in sleeping
- The uncontrollable feeling of worry
- Increased irritability
- Restlessness

People with a generalized anxiety disorder will experience these symptoms to extreme or persistent levels. A general anxiety disorder may manifest as vague, unsettling worry, or chronic anxiety that interferes with the daily routine.

Types of Anxiety Disorder: Panic Disorder

Sudden or brief attacks of severe apprehension and terror characterize the panic disorder. Panic attacks cause nausea, breathing problems, confusion, dizziness, and shaking. The attacks happen and escalate very fast, peaking after ten minutes. An attack might take up to several hours.

Symptoms

An attack usually emanates from a direct incident or trigger, but attacks can start randomly and suddenly with no clear cause. Panic attacks are assumed to emanate from an evolutionary reaction to harm.

Having these attacks is said to be intensely uncomfortable, frightening, and upsetting situations in a person's life.

A panic attack involves at least four of the below symptoms:

- Breathing problems, smothering feeling
- Tingling or numbness
- Sweating
- Trembling or shaking
- Choking Feelings
- Stomach upset and nausea

- Rapid heart rate, heart palpitations, or irregular heartbeat
- Feeling lightheaded or dizziness
- Experiencing a sudden intense fear of dying
- Discomfort and chest pain
- Feeling unusual hot and chills

An attack can also be linked with agoraphobia (a fear of places) where the patient assumes to be harmful and hard to escape from. A person who has experienced an attack usually says afterward that they felt trapped.

Causes of Panic Disorder

Panic and anxiety, to a particular extent, are an essential part of your survival instinct. However, when the levels of anxiety and panic get high that they impact the rational thought process negatively, a person normally gets afraid.

When your brain gets a surge of nervous signals—created to warn you of potential harm—the amygdala is stimulated. The amygdala regulates a person's anxious reaction.

Some people's amygdala responds to anxiety when there is no potential harm, causing that they will experience frequent panic attacks and high levels of anxiety.

When you receive a signal to respond to anxiety, your body will generate adrenaline (also called epinephrine).

A release of adrenaline to the body raises the heartbeat, provokes irregular breathing, churns the stomach, and causes profuse sweating.

If there is no imminent danger and the body is full of adrenalin, adrenalin will not be used. The build-up of adrenalin in a person's body can lead to a panic attack.

Some risk factors can maximize the probability of a person having a panic disorder and a panic attack:

- **Genetics May Play a Part:** If someone has a close relative, like a sibling or a parent with a panic disorder, they may be more prone to suffer a panic attack.
- **Family History:** Experiencing major life changes or stressful events can stimulate increased panic attacks and anxiety.
- **Behaviors:** Such as excessive alcohol drinking, large amounts of caffeine, or smoking are also risk factors related to panic attacks.

Would Cognitive-behavioral therapy be successful for anxiety? A significant first move to addressing this query is to consider the theory behind this form of therapy. Usually, CBT is practiced over a short amount of time and with a particular purpose in mind—unlike speech therapy or psychoanalysis that may continue for years. The goal is to change thoughts that underlie negative behaviors.

Cognitive-behavioral therapy is based on the premise that behaviors are responses to one's own thoughts rather than external events. We can isolate and unlearn our negative thoughts because they are learned. After we can establish a positive thinking pattern, our negative reactions will stop. Cognitive-behavioral therapy, under the supervision of a qualified practitioner, splits apart a major concern into tiny, more achievable issues. This enables the patient and therapist to work together to solve these smaller problems. For instance:

Jim is being a hypochondriac. He deals with day-to-day imaginary aches and pains. He often sees his doctor with new symptoms for which the doctor can see little cause; nonetheless, Jim remains convinced he has a life-threatening disease. Jim invests a lot of time on internet blogs, searching for more details about various signs and illnesses.

Jim and his CBT therapist would go through a process of isolating and articulating his negative thoughts, then putting in their place positive thoughts. This idea might come up to Jim and his therapist:

"The hurts and aches are just in my head. I realize my body is solid and stable as it has been fully checked out by my doctor. While I'm sure in my good and healthy heart, I'm also looking forward to returning to active life." I'm trying to let go of my symptoms because they're not in my body but in my head. Instead of only heading home and going to bed, I'm going to rejoice in my freshly discovered strenuousness.

This illustrates the process of replacing negative with positive thoughts to modify behavior, although it is an extremely optimistic example of this. It is easy to see that there is potential for anxiety cognitive-behavioral therapy to help the sufferer. Operating with a professional practitioner is crucial to making a CBT plan effective. People who suffer from anxiety also carry a lot of commitment to their convictions. What the trained professional will be coaxing the patient to do is try new and healthier ways of thinking. If it wasn't for that professional guidance, this kind of therapy would be extremely challenging.

So, is there a way of self-help to do anxiety cognitive-behavioral therapy? Strictly placed, no. But presenting approaches just like CBT is a popular response to a variety of self-help alternatives. Such a strategy should include:

- Determine negative thinking
- Recognize the imagined menaces are in your head—not true.
- Look for another positive strategy that leads to healthy habits.

It will be useful to understand the cognitive-behavioral therapy components as you consider your self-help options. Cognitive-behavioral therapy for anxiety may be costly, and a sufferer will choose to choose a self-help alternative for this and several other purposes. Search for solutions that reflect on the present dilemma (not alternatives that dig into a person's past) and solutions that allow the individual to shift towards healthy behavioral habits gradually and thoughtfully. Neither CBT nor the like are fast fixes. While Cognitive-behavioral therapy needs time and commitment for anxiety, it is not as extensive as certain other types of therapy. The cognitive-behavioral therapy for fears will and does function on many patients with commitment and perseverance.

Social Anxiety Disorder

Social anxiety disorder is also called social phobia. A phobia is an irrational fear of a particular environment, situation, or object.

Social anxiety disorder can involve a fear of being judged by other people.

Social anxiety disorder, in part, is focused on social phobia, which means a person has a fear of being judged by other people. The reason why an individual's social anxiety becomes a mental disorder is it manipulates the individual's thoughts, behaviors, and emotions. However, there are also unique factors that make up the person being treated. For example, a person's family history and personal experiences will play a role in that person's social anxiety.

The two main symptoms that a person with this condition will have are they will avoid social situations, or they will experience extreme anxiety when put into a social situation. The majority of the people who have social anxiety will feel as though something just is not right when in a social environment, but they cannot pinpoint what the problem is.

People with this disorder will be fearful of making a mistake or looking bad. As a result, they feel embarrassed and humiliated when in front of other people. Individuals with social anxiety disorder typically are aware that their thinking is irrational;

however, their mind does not allow them to overcome the irrational thoughts, and so the anxiety continues.

Social anxiety may also cause a person to have a twisted mindset to the point where they have false beliefs about the social situations they are in, and they may develop negative opinions about the people around them as a result.

Along with social phobia is the component of anticipatory anxiety. This occurs prior to a social event. The individual will become anxious about a social situation, days, and possibly even weeks before a social gathering takes place. This can prolong a person's fear of an event and lead them to withdraw from friends and family to cope with the anxiety.

Some of the noticeable symptoms that can arise during fear and anxiety for a social event include confusion, sweating, rapidly beating heart, stomach pain, diarrhea, shaking, and muscle tension. In children, the symptoms may also include crying, clinging to a parent, or having a tantrum. In both children and adults, if anxiety becomes severe enough, it can result in a panic attack.

A panic attack occurs when a person experiences a sudden feeling of discomfort that reaches its peak in a matter of minutes. Some of the more common symptoms of a panic attack include numbness and tingling, feeling detached from one's self, breath shortness, fast heart rate, dizziness, and nausea.

Due to the social anxiety symptoms and the possibility of a panic attack, these individuals tend to go into social situations with extreme distress, which may lead to them avoiding social gatherings altogether.

The most common situation that evokes anxiety—even though without the disorder—is public speaking. However, there is a multitude of situations that creates extreme anxiety, depending on the person. For example, some people show symptoms of social anxiety when having to use a public bathroom.

Other people become anxious when eating, drinking, performing a task, or writing while people are watching them. Going to a party, on a date, or flirting with someone new can also bring on social anxiety symptoms. Other situations include speaking to a person of authority, giving one's opinion, walking into a crowded room, making new friends, or speaking up in front of other people. Some people will find mild discomfort when put in these types of situations; however, the individual with social anxiety will find their thoughts, emotions, and behaviors consumed with their irrational fears when put in one of the above situations.

Studies have shown that about 48% of the people in the United States will display some degree of shyness. Another study from "Harvard Medical School" estimates that 12% of the American population will experience a social anxiety disorder in their lifetime. Percentage-wise, the numbers may seem small; however, when looking at the percentages in numbers, around 140 million people are affected, to some degree, by shyness in the United States, and 15 million people show signs of social anxiety disorder.

The disorder typically occurs around a person's adolescent years or young adulthood, yet it can also take place at any time in a person's lifetime. Some people will show symptoms as early as early childhood.

The reason behind the sporadic onset of social anxiety stems from the delicate blend of psychological, environmental, and behavioral factors in a person's life.

One possible psychological factor is a traumatic event in a person's past. If a person was once in a social situation that caused them anxiety or fear, this could result in fear of the future social situation. Some examples of traumatic events include being bullied, being humiliated by peers, or being embarrassed in front of a group of people.

A possible environmental factor that can lead to social anxiety is if an individual observes another person being traumatized and laughed at by other people. They will remember that person's actions and the results and then become fearful of the same outcome happening to them if put in another social situation.

Children who are not given the opportunity to be put into enough social situations or are overprotected by their parents are more likely to have their social skills stunted. As a result, healthy overall social development is sacrificed. It is also important to note that the children who are not given the opportunity to learn proper social skills are likely to have their social anxiety worsen over time.

The main biological factors for the onset of social anxiety include an abnormality of the brain. Studies have been done to suggest that an odd performance by some of the brain's circuits used to regulate fear and the "fight-or-flight" response occurs in some of the people with the disorder.

Another possible biological reason can be that the disorder is hereditary. If a parent, sibling, or one's own children show signs of social anxiety, then they are more likely to develop the disorder themselves.

Once a person is able to discern that they do have social anxiety, the next step is to learn how to treat it. Due to the fact that it is a mental disorder, the process of working through social anxiety will probably take time and a lot of effort. The most prominent enemy, when trying to fight social anxiety, is one's own mind.

When a person is put into a social situation where the environment or experience becomes negative, this can lead to the person developing negative beliefs and problematic behaviors. The mentioned beliefs and behaviors are what fuel social anxiety because of the shift in cognitive functioning it causes.

Some of the possible negative opinions that a person may have running through their mind about themselves can include thinking that they are unlikable. Even when someone else tells the person with social anxiety that they are liked, it can still be difficult to change the belief because the belief becomes exceedingly powerful.

Other possible thoughts can be anxiety about not knowing what to say in a given situation, that a person will not feel like they belong, they will say something stupid and thinking something is wrong with them. Oftentimes, negative beliefs are connected to a person's lack of self-esteem.

When a person has a diminished feeling of self-worth, it is easier for the negative thoughts to appear as the truth. A person with social anxiety will believe that they truly have nothing that they can offer in a social situation, and in turn, they avoid said situation.

At first, the person will lower the number of symptoms they are experiencing by avoiding different types of social interactions; however, they are also not allowing themselves to live a complete life and will lead to worsening symptoms when they are put into a social situation that they cannot avoid.

It is important to note that it is not only the fear of a social situation that causes people anxiety. People with social anxiety also tend to believe that they do not deserve to benefit from healthy and successful social interactions.

This is because of the negative mindset a person with social anxiety builds about themselves. A person will typically beat themselves up before going into a social situation in order to gain some level of control over the upcoming interaction.

Mentally attacking and pushing one's self down leads a person to reach a point where they cannot feel any lower about themselves. The goal here is to prevent other people from putting themselves down any further during social interaction. The individual may feel a sense of control as a result, yet the pain and suffering are far greater. It is also the main reason for a person's underdeveloped social life.

However, no matter how hopeless and undeserving a person may feel, there are treatment options that can aid in rebuilding a person's self-esteem and allow them to grow their social skills.

The main goal of any treatment option is to detangle the negative thoughts, behaviors, and emotions a person feels related to social interactions. This enables the individual to become alleviated from their suffering and the barriers that have prevented them from living their life to the fullest.

The treatment of social anxiety disorder has three primary goals. The first goal is to help the person identify their misconceptions about social situations so that healthier thoughts can take over. When a person is suffering from social anxiety, they have automatic negative thoughts that are at the forefront of their mind. These thoughts are considered the mind's trap. When a person is able to identify their individual mind traps, they are finding the foundation of their fear. An example is if a person with social anxiety is preparing for a presentation, they will have underlying thoughts such as, "I am going to embarrass myself" or "I am not going to know what I am talking about."

It can be nerve-racking to think about why one is afraid and why one thinks in a certain way about social interactions, but it is important to comprehend one's inner thoughts in order to overcome social anxiety.

Once the automatic inner thoughts have been identified, it becomes time to analyze them. Asking oneself questions such as "even if I don't know what I am talking about, will people actually notice?" and "Am I positive that I will embarrass myself?" The analysis of one's inner thoughts allows them to identify the types of unhealthy thinking patterns or mind traps they have developed.

The possible thinking patterns or mind traps that a person may develop include mind-reading. This occurs when one person jumps to conclusions about another person's thoughts, behaviors, or objectives without seeing if they are true. This is specifically true for social anxiety when the individual is thinking that other people are thinking bad thoughts about them. One example is thinking that the people around them are looking at the person with social anxiety and judging them as being strange or stupid.

Another possible thinking pattern or trap is catastrophic thinking, which means a person assumes that if a problematic event were to occur, the outcome would be horrific. A person with social anxiety would specifically focus on the possibility that if a negative event happens, they will not be able to handle the situation. They may also think about a difficult situation and think that there is no end to the event. One example is before a job interview, and a person begins thinking that if they become too nervous, they will not be able to remember everything they want to say, and they will not get the job.

The third option is when a person puts on metaphorical negative glasses. When this occurs, an individual is pulling basically all of their focus on the negatives while ignoring the positives of a given situation. Positive assets, accomplishments, and behaviors seem irrelevant to a person with social anxiety. The person may go as far as to telling themselves that their positive attributes do not matter. One example is if, during a business meeting, the person is focusing on the person who is looking out the window rather than seeing the other 20 heads who are listening intently to what is being said.

The final possible negative thinking pattern or mind trap is fortune-telling. This is when a person makes negative predictions about the future, specifically how a person will act or what the outcome of an event will be. The individual believes that the prediction will come true even though, rationally, the prediction is not likely to be accurate. An example of this will be if a person thinks, "if I lose this job, I will never find another one."

Once the negative thinking pattern or mind trap has been identified, the final step is to alter the negative automatic thoughts and transform them into more beneficial thoughts about oneself and possibly social interactions.

The second goal is to help the person control their anxiety by limiting their physical symptoms. When a person becomes anxious, there are changes that occur within their body, such as the speeding of their heart rate, sweating, irrational thinking, and breath shortness. However, there are techniques that can help a person to relax their body and reduce their physical response to anxiety.

When an individual's anxiety first beings to set in, they will experience shortness of breath, which leads to the person feeling suffocated, dizziness, and the tensing of muscles. If a person is able to learn how to regulate their breathing, then they will be able to control their physical sensations of anxiety.

The use of a breathing exercise can help a person to remain calm during situations that typically would cause them anxiety. First, the individual should find a comfortable place to sit so that their back is bent and their shoulders are relaxed. Next, place a hand on one's chest and the other onto one's stomach. Then inhale a slow and deep breath through the nose for four seconds. The hand on one's stomach should rise, but the hand on the chest should barely move at all. Hold the breath for two seconds once done inhaling.

Next, exhale the breath through one's mouth for six seconds. Expel as much air as possible during this portion of the exercise. The hand on the stomach should move during the exhale, but the hand on the chest should exhibit little movement.

Continue the process of breathing in through the nose and out through the mouth while focusing on the slow and steady pattern of inhaling for four seconds, holding that breath for two seconds, and exhaling as much air as possible for six seconds.

In addition to deep breathing exercises, a person may also choose to utilize other relaxation techniques such as yoga, muscle relaxation, and medication. Any of those techniques can help a person to gain self-control and learn to become more relaxed.

The final goal is to help the individual to stop avoiding social situations that have caused anxiety in the past. Facing one's fears of a social situation head-on is one of the most beneficial tools used to overcome anxiety.

Avoiding uncomfortable situations can become very appealing to a person who has social anxiety because they can provide short-term relief from negative thoughts. However, in the long term, avoidance does not allow a person to be able to learn how to cope with the stress that a social situation can cause. Actuality, the more a person tries to avoid social interactions, the more distressing future social situations become.

In other words, the more a person avoids their fears of social events, the more power the anxiety has over the person. Anxiety and confidence are extremely combative when they are put against one another, which means in order to lessen their anxiety, their confidence must first be built up.

Avoiding social interactions can also prevent a person from reaching their full potential or their goals. For example, if a person allows their fear of speaking up to stand in their way of voicing their creative thoughts in a meeting, this could be what stands in their way from getting the promotion they have worked so hard to reach.

At times, it can seem nearly impossible to face an intimidating social interaction, but a person can push through the fear and conquer the social situation if they take it one step at a time. Meaning, it is essential that a person faces their fears at a gradual and steady pace.

The best way to do so is to start with a situation the individual can handle and slowly work up to the more challenging aspects as time goes on. This will allow the individual to build their confidence and social abilities as they progress with facing their fears.

An example of how the process works could be if the idea of socializing with other people makes an individual nervous, they may start by attending a party with a close friend. Once the person becomes comfortable with the steps it takes to be at the party, they can work up to speaking with a stranger.

In order to reach one's success in overcoming social anxiety, the individual must remember to remain patient and not attempt to push towards a challenging situation until they are mentally ready to do so. It is not a smart idea to try to move through the process of overcoming anxiety too quickly, to try and take on too much or force any part of the process. This will actually make the anxiety worse in the end.

It can be extremely challenging to try to overcome social anxiety on one's own, but with the correct treatment and tools, a person can enjoy a fuller and happier life.

Someone with social phobia may be very fearful of embarrassment in social events. This fear can affect professional and personal relationships.

Social phobia usually happens early in childhood as a normal part of social development and may go unnoticed until the person is mature enough. The triggers and frequency of social phobia vary depending on the person.

Most people feel nervous in particular social events, such as taking part in a competition. It is normal and would not qualify as a social anxiety disorder.

Quick Facts about Social Anxiety

- Treatment can involve medication and psychotherapy.
- Those with social anxiety are disproportionately nervous in social events.
- Social anxiety disorder is more popular in women than in men.

Symptoms of Social Anxiety Disorder

They may be behavioral, physical, or emotional symptoms. Social anxiety disorder can influence your daily tasks, including work and education.

Emotional and behavioral symptoms include:

- A blank mind during social events cause anxiety
- Fear of meeting people in power or authority
- Panic attacks or severe anxiety when facing the feared event
- Excessive fear of embarrassment
- Fear of being in events with strangers
- Dread concerning how they will be introduced to other people

- Avoiding events where the person feels that they may be the center of attention

Physical symptoms and signs include:

- Dry throat and mouth
- Trembling and shaking
- Muscle tension
- Nausea
- Excessive sweating
- Cold hands and clammy
- Avoiding eye contact
- Abdominal pain
- Blushing
- Heart palpitations

A person experiencing social anxiety disorder may also:

- Be not assertive
- Have poor social skills
- Have a low self-esteem
- They talk negatively about themselves, with self-defeating and inaccurate thoughts
- Be oversensitive to criticism

Here are the causes of social anxiety disorder:

Chemicals in the Body System

Currently, scientists are researching which chemical components in the body might enhance the advancement of social anxiety disorder. Serotonin, a brain chemical, may play a major role when the amounts are not high. A person is compassionate.

Demographics and Weather

Countries in the Mediterranean have low rates of this disorder compared to the Scandinavian countries. This could be a fact because of the hot weather as well as the high population. The warm environment may minimize the avoidance of social situations and maximize contact with other people.

Genetics

The condition seems to run in families. Hence it could be inherited from one person to a close relative.

Effective Cognitive-Behavioral Therapy Techniques

Cognitive-behavioral therapy for a large population of Americans who suffer from personality disorders has been proven effective. This has been proved successful in managing drug misuse, social anxiety disorder, and post-traumatic stress, along with a number of other conditions. It is known that this form of therapy is progressive and goal-oriented. This specialty emphasizes establishing targets and attaining them throughout the life of the individual. In fact, several doctors believe that this is the single most effective therapy to alleviate the symptoms of social anxiety disorder.

The main purpose of this form of therapy is to question the deeply rooted beliefs of the patient, which triggers negative and crippling behavior. If a psychiatrist or therapist may alter a person's response to anxiety-promoting pain, then the individual can be encouraged to cope and even develop new strategies for dealing with it. It's all about convincing the victim why their thinking processes—at least the way they experience things—really don't exist. Thus this discovery will allow them to recognize the need for a transition.

You don't want to interact with them intellectually as you want to treat those with an anxiety disorder. Instead, you appeal to their emotions and first-reaction responses. Therefore, something more intensive than just a heart-to-heart conversation may be needed to change negative behavior.

For cognitive-behavioral therapy, two common techniques include gradual exposure and systematic desensitization. The first of these entails a psychiatrist or therapist addressing one of their most dreaded triggers to an individual. For example, when addressing social anxiety, this fear may simply be speaking in front of a large number of people. The doctor forces this confrontation but ensures it takes place in an organized, sensitive, and highly supervised manner so that the patient is not overwhelmed. The second involves simulating the actual experiences and addressing the emotions.

Cognitive-Behavioral and Drug Therapy

If you have an anxiety condition, a simple concern you can ask yourself is: "How am I getting better?" If you ever bring that up to the doctor, they are more likely to recommend your medication without ever considering the most efficient, clinically proven medicine around: Cognitive-behavioral therapy or CBT. Scientists have discovered several principles over the past 20 or 30 years or so that help people overcome their fears. These principles have to do with how thinking affects or colors emotional responses and how specific behaviors either contribute to emotional responses that are helpful and adaptive or painful and difficult. These principles helped form a new type of therapy called Cognitive-behavioral therapy.

The cognitive part (meaning thinking) works by teaching people to transform harmful, overly fearful, and unrealistic anxious thinking into more positive and realistic ways of thinking. The underlying hypothesis is: If you change the way you think, the way you feel will change. The behavioral part works by encouraging people to engage in activities that have a calming effect of alleviating nervous anxiety and having to face new experiences, rather than suppressing concerns through a cycle of emotional adjustment to fears. In reducing anxiety and preventing relapse, cognitive-behavioral approaches for anxiety disorders are superior to medication. Even most Americans have never learned about it, and because other physicians may not have immediate exposure to this method, psychological problems are still tested for treatment.

Find the key types of medications used to 'treat' psychological problems. There are two main classes of medicines most commonly prescribed for anxiety treatment: Tranquilizers (a class or group of Benzodiazepine-based medicines such as Xanax,

Ativan, and Valium) and antidepressants (such as Prozac, Paxil, Zoloft, and Wellbutrin. Recent research suggests that while benzodiazepine medicines work faster, there are many issues associated with their use (including a rebound in addiction and anxiety when discontinued). The honest fact is that medications are often correlated with a number of adverse side effects: weight gain, sexual arousal (such as trouble attaining pleasure and lack of desire), dry mouth, vomiting, stomach problems, and much more. Gaining weight and developing sexually disordered are especially normal among them. Another big issue for these types of anxiety illness substance care is that if the medication is discontinued, the odds of regression are far higher than with a good course of cognitive-behavioral therapy; simple truth is, drugs only work while you're taking them! When you are developing new coping strategies from CBT, they can become a part of you for the remainder of your life resulting in substantially decreased distress long when therapy is finished.

Cognitive-behavioral approaches to emotional issues have been repeatedly demonstrated in a variety of well-controlled studies by rigorous scientific studies to significantly reduce panic, anxiety, worry, and fear. With certain anxiety conditions (including panic disorder and agoraphobia), it has also been proven that such treatments provide stronger results and much fewer relapses than treatment (again, after you stop the medicine, the effects typically come back at some point). Many individuals remain ignorant of these effects as medicine is now by far the most successful therapy for anxiety disorders. Unfortunately, medication doesn't teach skills per above! Brain imaging studies have shown that they experienced a decrease in the brain's fear center after people underwent a course of Cognitive-behavioral therapy!

Cognitive-Behavioral Therapy to Treat Autism

Several coping interventions for handling individuals with autism have been tried from time to time. Pivotal response training and an analysis of applied behaviors are among the most common. But, it is likely that adults, older children, and adolescents will benefit more from cognitive-behavioral therapy, another major treatment intervention for autism.

Many efforts have been made to develop Cognitive-behavioral therapy for troubled adolescents and older children. Typically, the focus has been on people who still struggle with fear, as this is a specific characteristic of autism. The challenge was to find out if autistic children have the skills needed to be a success in Cognitive-behavioral therapy. Fortunately, the response is in the affirmative. A 2012 research measured and contrasted the executive skills of older children with autism with those of non-autistic children. Nearly every child in the former group possessed cognitive-behavioral abilities and could distinguish feelings, behaviors, and thoughts. They only found emotions hard to recognize.

Traditional cognitive-behavioral therapy calls for strong language and abstract thinking capabilities, and for those with autism, this is often a challenge. Researchers noticed this and changed the intervention to fit individuals with autism, such as making things more physically pleasing and physical and repeated. For example, simply asking the children to rank their anxiety orally on a scale of 1 to 10, a therapist may have a thermometer showing the anxiety level from low to high, and asking the participants to indicate the prop to illustrate this. Another strategy for autism in Cognitive-behavioral therapy involves focusing on a child's talent and special interests that help keep the child motivated and engage, building frequent sensory activities and movement breaks for those who may have under or over-reactivity attention deficit problems.

The researchers noted that cognitive-behavioral therapy needs to address social skills among those with autism, as core social deficits among young people with autism contribute to anxiety that then intensifies the teens' social problems. The therapy can be implemented in various ways, including families, individuals, groups, and even families and groups alike. Community meetings have the benefit of seeing many people with autism dealing with the same problems and trying to overcome them together. Social help and intimacy acquired through the cycle may in itself be therapeutic.

A family behavioral autism intervention also involves parents who are learning themselves about the challenges facing their babies. It also means training them to promote the usage of cognitive-behavioral therapy strategies anytime the infant is faced with a real-life circumstance. This will make them feel optimistic and excited about leading to a meaningful difference in a child's life.

Researchers found the problem of protecting children from a possible negative experience is often a tough call for most parents to make. Autistic children typically have a background of real-world behavioral and emotional problems, including frustrating setbacks. Sometimes, their parents are hesitant to subject the infant to more mistakes and unwittingly restrict the access to activities required to become less insecure and more confident.

Cognitive-Behavioral Therapy (CBT), for Adults with Autism or Asperger

Adults with a diagnosis of Asperger's syndrome or autism can find it especially challenging to control emotions. Cognitive-behavioral therapy, commonly referred to as CBT, can be a successful way to cope with mental health problems, including unpleasant emotions such as depression, repetitive thoughts, or anxiety.

Many adults with Asperger's, ADHD, or ASD fear the thought of visiting a psychotherapist. The idea of examining past relationships, thinking about memories in early childhood, and focusing on feelings may seem repetitive, meaningless, or unpleasant. They can imagine a therapy session as something like what Freud did (or Woody Allen on a sofa), and the therapist nods and talks about fantasies. And they imagine a stereotyped entertainment psychiatrist demanding again and again, "What did that make you feel?" It's not shocking with these counseling photos that many people may choose to cope with their emotional pain rather than seeing a psychiatrist.

But there are other possibilities!

Therapy can be far more realistic and goal-oriented than such videos that would lead you to think, and that's just what concerns many adults with Asperger's or autism. And that is where CBT is coming in.

CBT is based on the idea that our feelings (or cognitions) and perceptions are associated with our behaviors. We can determine how these thoughts trigger depressed or anxious feelings or behaviors by becoming aware of our thoughts, examining them, and analyzing them. You should check the theories behind the thinking for false logic or wrong generalizations. Because several people with autism or Asperger's thrive at critical reasoning, it may be rather normal to analyze their own feelings for illogical trends.

CBT handles emotions but in a concrete manner. Emotions are discussed and often explained in-depth so that they can be understood better. Most CBT therapists have customer rates and calculate their feelings as a way to be more conscious of them. How the body experiences its emotion can be explored. The hope is that clear knowledge of the feelings, how they behave, and what roles they perform will make it simpler for people to control them. Again, for those on the autism spectrum, this practical and precise approach may feel very natural.

Do not equate CBT with ABA, please. ABA, or applied behavior analysis, is often called behavior therapy—but it is not cognitive-behavioral therapy. ABA is a specific therapy to teach new behaviors, often used on autistic children. It is not psychotherapy; it is not about emotions or issues such as depression, anxiety, or repetitive thinking. CBT may include a behavioral pattern, such as setting up a regular workout program as part of symptom management, but it is not about giving small incentives to adults any time they meet the demands of the therapist. Cognitive-behavioral therapy and cognitive therapy are also somewhat ambiguous. Cognitive therapy is, strictly speaking, one type of therapy that falls under the umbrella of more general CBT types. In practice, most clinicians interchangeably use the terms "cognitive therapy" and "cognitive-behavioral therapy."

Ready to try out CBT? Most clinicians will not identify themselves as CBT clinicians because, where necessary, they may use certain strategies. To find a therapist who is familiar with Asperger's and autism and one who really enjoys working on the autism spectrum with the individual is probably more important. Tell your potential therapist that you are interested in a more practical and concrete approach, define the goals you are looking for, and ask them to use CBT on a regular basis.

Chapter 4: Cognitive-Behavioral Therapists

For example, cognitive-behavior therapy will use resources from the cognitive-behavioral therapy (CBT) toolkit, and a cognitive-behavioral therapist's approach will be focused on the principles of the CBT toolkit.

Cognitive-behavioral therapy is based on the idea that our emotions, including people, situations, and incidents, affect our feelings and behaviors, not external things. The advantage of this idea is that even if the external situation doesn't improve, we will change the way we perceive so that we behave and act better.

I think it was a Stoic philosopher, Marcus Aurelius, who said it this way; "it's not the event that causes our feelings, it's our attitude towards the event that causes our feelings."

If I can adjust my mindset toward the situation, then I can change my feelings.

A cognitive-behavioral consultant will then help clients discover particular thoughts or thought cycles that cause uncomfortable feelings, and those feelings will trigger actions that then create unexpected outcomes.

Cognitive-behavioral therapy may help a client dispute what is referred to as an irrational thought, or maybe discover evidence for and against a "hot thought," and then form a balanced interpretation of the external situation that leaves the inner feeling situation more balanced.

Such "hot thoughts" can fall into a sequence or may have other language components and include phrases such as "may, should, or must," and a cognitive behavior specialist may help you learn how to refute either the trend or the terminology as the thought arises.

A cognitive-behavioral therapist will be more of a directive, and the work duration will be short-term.

A cognitive-behavioral therapist will not be interested in developing a relationship style centered on a Rogerian person, although the relationship will certainly be cordial.

I think that the emerging brain fitness model is good for a cognitive-behavioral therapist to sell because it can be helpful for a client to see their work as part of what they need to do to grow new brain cells.

Physical exercise, nutrition, including antioxidants and omega-3 fatty acids, good sleep, stress management, and book learning experiences are the pillars of brain fitness.

Fast negative thoughts and negative thinking habits, such as "all or nothing thinking," will fill the body with stress hormones in the 1/18th second we talked about earlier, and a bath of excessive stress hormones allows neurogenesis or the growth of new brain cells extremely difficult.

I think everyone agrees with Dr. Daniel Amen's feeling that when it comes to the brain, a cognitive-behavioral therapist should tell their client that attending to the pillars of brain fitness can be very beneficial for every area of their life, as the brain is involved in everything we do.

As a user of cognitive-behavioral tools in my anger management groups and brain fitness groups, I like to have my clients use tools like the "dual n-back task" and "heart rate variability biofeedback" to get an impression of how meaningfully they can manage attention, memory, the time between heartbeats and even IQ.

When clients see themselves developing expertise in those areas, they can then have their cognitive-behavioral therapist tackle cognitions with greater confidence.

We have about 60,000 thoughts a day, I read elsewhere, and we should know that a lot of them represent us.

Dr. Aaron Beck's approach to applied behavioral therapy helps people change their lives

The cognitive-behavioral treatment has been commonly implemented and scientifically validated as a successful method of psychotherapy in more than 400 studies. Dr. Aaron Beck has been practicing cognitive-behavioral counseling for over 50 years and has founded a center to educate practitioners to support people to tackle a broad variety of psychiatric problems involving paranoia, anxiety, and depression. Cognitive-behavioral therapy has gained much support from the psychological field and is a hands-on, patient-empowering form of therapy that addresses the patient's current emotions and thinking patterns. In the past, the counseling profession has been primarily involved in a patient's past encounters as a key to unlocking their potential. Dr. Beck's cognitive-behavior therapy suggests that there are certain keys in our world.

Cognitive-behavioral therapy succeeds when each patient has an individualized blueprint and target structure that will help them visualize their recovery route. It works on assuming that each person has a different process of thinking associated with every circumstance in life. E.g., when one individual might see a "cause" like a fire truck and respond with excitement thinking, "I hope there is no disaster," another individual might instantly panic and take on the mentality of "oh no one has certainly died or lost their home to a fire." These two separate responses place in motion entirely opposing influences on the person's intellectual, physical, and emotional facets. What many people fail to realize is that those assumptions or perceptions dictate their life course. In other terms, the way we feel and think today determines our truth and our life.

Another great CBT feature is that it does not give patients Band-Aid approaches and rather encourages them to create different ideas and values themselves (with psychological assistance), which can enable them to be successful and solve the challenges they encounter. Such self-help techniques should be found in various life conditions where our "gridiron value" framework or "opinions" are so strongly rooted that they trigger both automatic and emotional reactions.

Dr. Beck was a pioneer in the field of cognitive behavior. The first trial was on his own, where he explored the approaches that were grounded in logical relational counseling to shape what is now known as cognitive-behavioral therapy. He also participated in a clinical trial and found that CBT is just as effective as medication in treating mental illnesses, such as depression, which are often difficult to overcome. On this widely prescribed method of counseling, he founded "the Beck Center for Cognitive Behavior Therapy" and continues to support patients and train therapists.

CBT should be prescribed for heart attacks, anxiety, psychological problems, stress, and control conflict as a way to help resolve destructive thoughts over a lifetime. Patients need to be very committed to the process and be mindful of specific goals. One of the first questions that a patient needs to ask themselves before starting CBT is, "What do I want to change, and what do I want to gain from therapy?" While some patients may start CBT because of mental illness, others use it as a way to gain abundance in their lives' areas where they feel they are lacking or stuck in a negative cycle.

Beck's cognitive behavior therapy begins with patients tackling their own beliefs and thinking processes with the help of a trained therapist (for example, several therapists in Huntington Beach are actively practicing Beck's CBT therapy. If you are specifically confronted with rationalizing these things and evaluating your respondent's behavior, you can take steps to change them.

Cognitive-behavioral therapy is meant to change reality. People are required to bring their learning into their daily lives to test their new perceptions and witness the amazing results on their own. CBT has fundamentally changed the face of psychotherapy, and Dr. Aaron Beck has been a visionary, strongly trusting in the long-term benefits and self-help resources it offers to individuals.

How to Find a Good CBT Therapist

Evidence suggests that CBT is currently the most effective treatment for a range of mental health issues, including depression, anxiety, eating disorders, OCD, PTSD. As such, it is recommended by "the National Institute for Clinical Excellence (NICE)," and therefore, by the government as the treatment of choice. Despite the recent introduction of IAPTs (Improving Access to Psychological Therapies), however, the government is initiating to ensure that CBT is provided to all who need it, NHS waiting lists are still up to 12 months in length. As a result, patients are frequently finding care in the private sector, but the term "CBT Therapist" is not legally licensed, and practice is not limited, which ensures that anybody may provide CBT irrespective of credentials or experience. This leaves many people in need of the best treatments given out by the most experienced practitioners. So the following instructions should be observed in finding a CBT Therapist:

1. Look for a doctor for treatment and counseling. They have been qualified for doctoral or master's degrees for seven to nine years to enable people to resolve their relational problems. They'll be trained to use a wide variety of therapeutic techniques, one of which is CBT.
2. Ensure that the clinical/counseling psychologist holds a certificate of practice with "The British Psychological

Society," which is the UK psychology and psychology representative body. The Society was created in 1901 and had over 45,000 members. The Society is charged with supervising psychology and psychologists through its "Royal Charter." It is responsible for developing, promoting, and enforcing pure and applied psychology for the public good. Practical certificates are issued only to "chartered psychologists," which for psychologists is the standard of professional recognition. It represents the knowledge and expertise to the highest standards.

3. Ensure that the clinical/counseling Consultant is licensed with the "Board of Health Professionals," which oversees and controls health care professionals' work.

4. Make sure the "British Association for Cognitive and Behavioral Psychotherapies (BABCP)" accredits the clinical/counseling psychologist to practice. The BABCP is the lead organization in the UK for cognitive-behavioral therapy theory, practice, and development. "BABCP Accreditation" is the "Gold Standard" to which every CBT professional aims. Any practitioner may be a member, but accreditation with the BABCP shows that the practitioner has met the rigorous criteria outlined in their core profession, qualifications, and clinical experience, and ensures that their skills are continuously updated and developed through ongoing training.

Cognitive-Behavioral Therapy—An Effective Method to Beat Mental Disorders

A slight shift in perspective in our lives allows us to appreciate and resolve difficult circumstances. The way we behave and how we react to circumstances depends primarily on our outlook on life and conditions that explicitly or indirectly affect our lifestyle.

Cognitive-behavioral therapy, as a psychotherapeutic approach, helps individuals learn new skills in dealing with dysfunctional behaviors and emotions. A form of treatment is used for patients as well as communities to help them heal from addictions, depressions, heart attacks, nervous problems, and other phobias. In such therapy programs, the self-help sessions help understand and overcome various disorders and alleviate symptoms. Such CBT is beneficial in most cases for patients suffering from various mental health disorders and depressions, as it poses fewer risks than antidepressants and other psychotherapy methods do.

To use the best solutions through CBT for any type of mental disorder, individuals should feel free to expose their worries, problems, or fears. It allows CBT professionals to offer better advice and recommend long-term benefits of the appropriate treatment or plan. They take the initiative in understanding the disease and its severity, which can vary from person to person. The therapy focuses on eliminating the negative behavior by systematic processes used on individuals of different age groups. Such treatment has also proven a blessing for those who suffer from:

- Post-traumatic stress disorder
- Insomnia
- Anxiety
- Eating problems
- Obsessive-compulsive disorders

In the early 1960s, the idea of cognitive-behavioral therapy was formed as a mixture of behavioral and cognitive therapy, focuses on the beliefs and emotions which affect an individual's mood and attitude. The counseling improves one's thought process, makes it safer and more resilient, and helps alter dysfunctional behavior habits. Any current or personal interactions affect one's understanding of any particular circumstance. This perspective is always skewed, and therefore one responds with an emotional reaction to circumstances. The very first move in CBT is to educate people with full clarification to evaluate the problems and circumstances to follow the correct and acceptable response. CBT or Cognitive-behavioral therapy provided by clinicians aims to provide people with meaningful recovery from physical and mental reactions related to upsetting conditions. This counseling comes to play as a person analyzes, interprets, and controls their thoughts actively. When feelings and opinions are interwoven, people have greater power over their emotions. Anyone who desires to monitor their learning flow will use this strategy to gain full benefits.

CBT, although a protracted process, is very effective and, therefore, worth all the effort. This is also an extremely common recovery plan that helps patients heal from a broad spectrum of conditions from insomnia, panic disorder to bulimia. Look for such specialists in CBT therapy if you are looking for a sure solution to your stress, disorders, or depressions. They will direct you to be more optimistic in life, quickly relieving you from all kinds of anxieties.

Obsessive-Compulsive Disorder Diagnosis with Cognitive-Behavioral Therapy

When a patient is diagnosed with OCD or obsessive-compulsive disorder, a mixture of antidepressant medications and psychological therapy is used in the standard form of treatment. Although there are several types of psychiatric treatment, "CBT" or "cognitive-behavioral therapy" is the most effective for managing OCD.

Cognitive-behavioral therapy centers on the idea that our emotions or beliefs influence how we respond or behave and not our climate, experiences, or circumstances. Thus, by modifying the way we feel, we will also improve the way we react to these circumstances.

CBT—The Avoidance of Detection and Reaction

The exposure-response prevention strategy used in cognitive-behavioral therapy is used to help the patient gain control over their compulsions by introducing them to their obsessions and then preventing their compulsive behavior.

For example, if an individual has the compulsion of washing hands very excessively, they are asked to shake hands or touch an object like a doorknob and then refrain from washing their hands. This method has proved effective as the compulsive urge tends to go away on its own after a relatively short period.

Following some period after practicing this desensitization process, the individual starts to understand that they no longer have to operate out of their compulsions to relieve their distress. This type of cognitive-behavioral therapy was effective in reducing some of the compulsions in OCD patients and even eliminating them. The individual often knows how to control their intrusive emotions or obsessions and alleviate their distress by facing up all their fears.

Cognitive OCD Treatment

For people with obsessive-compulsive disorder, the treatment used works on the repetitive emotions that lead the client to indulge in their compulsive conduct. The unreasonable or unfounded feelings are tested by making the individual consider the statistics or the likelihood that their expectations may eventually become a fact.

When the individual has begun to recognize their negative feelings, they are shown the potential to substitute them with healthy and more optimistic thinking, as well as calming strategies that may be utilized to settle down in conditions that have already caused fear.

In most cases, people with obsessive-compulsive disorder may continue making a difference with only a few cognitive-behavioral therapy sessions. However, if you suffer from OCD syndrome, you may want to make sure you have a psychiatrist that is skilled in this sort of treatment to handle anxiety problems because not all practitioners are educated or certified in cognitive-behavioral therapy.

It has been found that receiving years of therapy that is inadequate to treat mental conditions is not uncommon for many individuals with OCD and has been known to exacerbate the symptoms in certain individuals with OCD. Therefore, you must research the therapist's qualifications and inquire about their level of experience in the treatment of anxiety disorders—if you are looking for a therapist to treat your OCD.

How will Cognitive-Compartmental Treatment Benefit OCD Sufferers?

Many people suffering from obsessive-compulsive disorder (OCD) have been led to numerous studies and research, most of which aim to find ways of treating, if not curing. Cognitive-behavioral therapy (CBT) is one of the most common recovery strategies performed today. This therapy is a form of psychotherapy that in addressing how an individual feels does capitalize on the value of thinking.

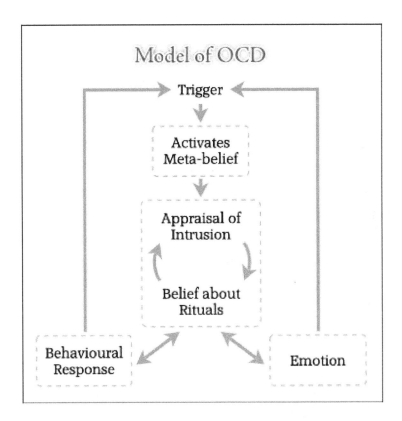

CBT is the general term for any therapeutic technique using the subconscious—rational, emotional therapy, rational life therapy, dielectic-behavioral therapy, cognitive therapy, and rational-behavior therapy are common examples of this. While these forms of therapies are special to each other in terms of individual results, some of these therapy features are similar across everyone.

The idea that all cognitive-behavioral therapies are based on the cognitive model of emotional response is one common characteristic for everyone. This means that the therapy focuses on the principle that all our feelings and behaviors are modeled internally; it also implies that they are caused by our thoughts and not by any pressure or influence from the environment. The conclusion to this is that the way we think about the situation can be changed, even though situations may not change.

Another aspect of the therapies is their brevity. All cognitive-behavioral therapies would only need to complete a maximum of 16 sessions. This is made possible by making the patient fully understand the nature of their condition and putting an end to the therapy at a specified time agreed by the therapist and the patient. This behavioral training makes the patient more helpful towards the therapeutic target, and all experts agree that this is, in essence, what OCD therapies most need is its patients' cooperation.

All CBTs also revolve around the principle of making the patient believe they can think differently through rational, self-counseling skills for the therapy to be effective and efficient. It is a collaboration between the CBT psychiatrist and the individual suffering from OCD. The therapist's role involves expressing concern for the sufferer's condition, listening to their woes, teaching them how to get through the whole process, and encouraging them to have every ability to succeed in the therapy.

To make the recovery process more efficient, CBT also includes giving the sufferer assignments and readings from which they can learn how to do self-control and how to privately practice the neutralizing activities they are encouraged to perform when their obsessions compel them to perform OCD rituals. Throughout that way, CBT is, by far, the most rising OCD therapy among multiple OCD sufferers in terms of prevalence and choice.

Can Cognitive-behavioral therapy help control anger?

As we choose to make our lives more up-to-date and time-sensitive, we end up piling on endless chores to fit into our limited 24-hour timetable. What we are left to do is seek and do anything within a short time frame, doing nearly everything and all in a single day. We just want to win, know, and have fun 'together' and not understand the aftermaths sometimes.

Stress, frustration, and resentment all derive from our no-idle time habits. Yes, this occurs in the world. With rising every day, we're recording a growing array of violent events. The number of angry children, angry parents, angry spouses, angry bosses, and angry workers are unstoppably increasing. And, 'anger' has been passed down through generations. Yeah, it's practically impossible to fathom when this would end.

While a range of therapeutic strategies is being utilized to address this situation and curtail that number of angry people, cognitive-behavioral therapy or CBT offers the best results, especially when it comes to treating behavioral problems like frustration. Rage is a question of actions but also a normal human emotion. We become mad when something that occurs doesn't match our ideal expectations or happens as a consequence of ongoing negative emotions of low self-esteem, envy, disappointment, violence, or vulnerability to life-threatening conditions. Accidents happen when you lose control in an angry moment. We can, instead, apply for the medication. One may never see the need to go in for therapy, either, because we feel that it is going to develop out of itself or it would make one feel very weak. But care must never be withheld or delayed, no matter what the reason might be.

Cognitive-behavioral therapy looks for a clear change in a patient's thought pattern. Anger comes as a result of negative emotions. Cognitive-behavioral therapy helps control the generation of negative emotions and events that cause such emotions, and anger will never again find a place in a person's life.

Cognitive-behavioral therapy adopts a variety of approaches and systems to help fix an individual's behavioral problems. Many of the most widely applied methods include Acceptance and Commitment Therapy, Cognitive-behavioral Assessment, Reduction of Exposure and Reaction, Multimodal Therapy, Problem-Solving Therapy, Moral Emotional Behavior Therapy, and others that rely primarily on stimulation and assertiveness. Behavioral Cognitive Therapy involves:

- Identifying conduct problems
- Identifying the triggers of negative feelings which lead to behavioral problems
- Developing ways to curb negative sentiments
- Developing alternative behavioral habits and reactions
- Exercising
- Addressing the source of unpleasant feelings and modifying a person's mental structure to prevent a relapse

Through cognitive-behavioral therapy, frustration can be properly controlled and handled. This is only by entrusting the psychiatrist and counselor that you will be able to comfortably handle this incredibly stressful circumstance. However, if you often feel awkward seeing a therapy specialist, you can find "computerized CBT" through which you communicate with a computer app installed or via voice-activated phone service rather than a human. All we need in most situations is to communicate our innermost thoughts to another, then let them be a therapist or a machine. The cure is all that counts.

Cognitive-Behavioral Therapy and Anxiety Management

There is a variety of solutions accessible for those searching for ways of managing fear that can be deemed "normal." What do such natural methods of relieving anxiety involve? These are anti-anxiety approaches that do not require the use of prescription pills or medications as a means to alleviate the issue. These methods often prove far healthier than what the overused anxiety treatment methods deliver. Cognitive-behavioral counseling is one such way of managing fear.

Cognitive-behavioral therapy isn't new. It has been used for decades by mental health professionals as a way of changing a person's behavioral decisions that produce mental health problems. In addition to being used as a way of reducing fear, cognitive-behavioral counseling has also been employed to address many extremely severe mental health conditions. What does cognitive counseling entail then? Here's a brief rundown of what's involved:

Cognitive-behavioral therapy, as a form of anxiety relief, involves taking a two-pronged approach to the problem. The first part involves tackling the cognitive issues that create anxiety. That is, they should analyze the thoughts and psychological components of the issue. It will examine the mental triggers that cause anxiety and then take steps to reverse the trigger effect.

The other side of the coin is the behavior therapy aspect for managing anxiety. This approach addresses the actual triggers associated with physical actions or activities, which may cause an anxiety-based reaction. As with the cognitive therapy mental portion, the purpose of behavioral therapy is to change one's response to anxiety-causing behaviors.

You may have legitimate questions regarding whether or not this form of treatment will contribute to significant outcomes when it comes to managing anxiety. There's nothing to worry about because cognitive-behavioral therapy has long been proven to be an effective treatment method. This is not a new clinical approach as it has been practiced for many years to great success by psychiatrists and other mental health professionals.

One of the key explanations that cognitive-behavioral counseling acts as a way to improve one's capacity to achieve much needed emotional relief focuses on the reality that most people don't realize what triggers their emotions. In a stunning number of instances, the person experiencing the problem is completely unknown to the triggers that cause their anxiety onset, stress, or a panic attack. The ability to get to the core of what creates the anxiety is made possible through working with a therapist. From this, it is easier to resolve fear, as it recognizes the source of the problem.

It's an almost difficult challenge to conquer fear by going to the root and raising the tension off your life. If you wish to feel freedom from fear, you would need to take care of all the issues that bring you tension and distress in your life.

Techniques for Cognitive-Behavior Treatment and Depressive Disorder

Cognitive-behavioral counseling is talk therapy that explores the thinking pattern of the person and the feelings related to certain thoughts. In anticipation of discovering a successful solution that either encourages more constructive behavior or reduces pessimistic behavior, both the person and the psychiatrist discuss certain feelings.

Cognitive-behavioral therapy is useful at coping with present challenges because it will not dive too far into previous concerns. Compared with many forms of treatment, it is often fairly short-term. As early as the fourth visit, tangible improvement may be made when the individual and psychiatrist discover a form of therapy that works.

An example of an intervention technique is addressing negative thoughts automatically. Imagine your boss walking up to your desk, neutrally and says, "I need to see you in my office for a private discussion in 10 minutes." What's the first thought that comes to mind? If it is "oh, I have to be in trouble," then it would be automatic negative thinking. The problem happens when there is no real rationale for these thoughts, and they cause overwhelming stress and anxiety to the point where you have visible coping problems. In this case, if the manager always talked directly about others while they were in distress and followed a common strategy, it would be a reasonable idea.

However, if the idea progresses to "he's going to fire me today, it might not be fair. I know that. Because I'm sure he has disliked me before," particularly if you've never been in trouble and no other proof suggests that your employer has a disdain for you. Those thought cycles should not be infrequent for people with bipolar illness suffering anxiety or depression. Such feelings may usually conflict with sleep and functions. So, disturbed sleep can facilitate harmful behavior for people with bipolar illness and may also cause a psychotic or depressive period.

A cognitive-behavioral counseling practitioner might ask the person to write down the thinking and examine it with the following questions:

1. Is this real?
2. How can I prove this concept is true?
3. Why do I react to this thought?
4. Without the thought, where will I be?

The counselor should introduce those questions to the psychiatrist to address the consequences and what should be changed if the unconscious critical thinking was not confirmed.

The added benefit to these cognitive-behavioral therapy techniques is that they will help people see the depressive episode approaching and understand how to best respond to it. If there are more involuntary depressive feelings, the individual may continue searching for the other signs and causes. They can provide this information to loved ones and to the therapist to see if adjustments to the lifestyle or other treatments are needed.

That is just one example of cognitive conduct therapy. Many other interventions and methods are using a similar style and requiring the patient to do these kinds of self-examination and return the results for analysis. Cognitive-behavioral therapy will help people handle their moods more easily as long as the depressive individual can do the research.

Cognitive-Behavioral Therapy and Alcohol Addiction

Addiction can take many forms: Depression, substance abuse, addiction to gambling, and so on. The list continues. The question that needs to be answered is how to eliminate those addictions? Nowadays, with the technological revolution, electronic drug recovery sessions, video therapy, and other care methods are available. The twelve-step method founded by the creators of Alcoholics Anonymous is one of the best therapies for addiction. However, other recovery services are being conducted in these modern days, such as the so-called "Cognitive-behavioral therapy," where a person undergoes because they wish to stay sober.

Cognitive-behavioral therapy (CBT) is a part of a psychotherapy group that puts focuses on the way an individual feels. It follows that what's on the mind of the person can profoundly affect the individual's behavior and feelings. Several cognitive-behavioral counseling services include logical life counseling, reasonable-emotional behavioral therapy, cognitive therapy, logical-behavioral therapy, and dialectical behavioral therapy.

Today, CBT is used in the care of depression and drug misuse. This functions as follows:

 It is based on asking questions (Socrates method).

In cognitive-behavioral therapy, the emotional response is given importance, in which the belief that is changing the way a client thinks will make that person feel better and act better (e.g., if the client thinks of staying clean for a year, then that will be done successfully).

In CBT, the client and the psychiatrist will communicate harmoniously and support one another for the effectiveness of the therapy

In CBT, clients feel they are in charge as their behaviors are designed to be evaluated, and they would be the ones to make choices about the measures they should follow. When they believe a mistake has been made, then it is up to them to fix it.

Reasonable-emotional-behavioral therapy (REBT) is the most widely used CBT program which battles addiction. This focuses on providing approaches to behavioral and emotional issues and challenges in existence that are intended to contribute to a satisfied and happy person.

REBT introduces neurological perturbation to change the A-B-C model. The model believes that the values people believe in are the main reasons why people become depressed, and they are the cause for the adversities the alcoholics or opioid users encounter. Clients are taught in this model to examine the things they believe in and do their best to turn those beliefs into something that would yield positive results.

Take note that REBT is deemed a short intervention to address particular problems. More complex issues require lengthy counseling. The REBT practitioner helps the client develop themselves through hard work that would also assist the client in coming trials and challenges. After the treatment, the patient is expected to feel both self-acceptance and recognition of life realities.

It is said that cognitive-behavioral therapy may be used to treat severe depression and addiction problems. Its structured teaching method is aimed at improving the way patients handle life. It is also an efficient means of changing the client's way of thinking about alcohol.

Chapter 5: The Mystery of Fibromyalgia and How Cognitive-Behavioral Therapy Can Help

Fibromyalgia syndrome (FMS) is the psychiatric term used to represent a complex clinical symptom disorder characterized by soft tissue pain, stiffness, and impaired tolerance of deep pain with psychological repercussions. It can resemble or follow signs of joint damage, but it is not a disease of arthritis or neurology. The disease impacts three to six million individuals—or as much as one in fifty Americans. Of those diagnosed with fibromyalgia, about 80 and 90% are women.

Typically, there is an emotional overlay of depression and anxiety, which affects the sufferer. There are many reasons for that to be true. Fibromyalgia has been overlooked as a bona fide illness by many within the medical community. Patients were told to overdramatize their pain and psychologically induced the stiffness or soreness. Others were advised the illness was fabricated for sympathy or interpreted as feigned helplessness by the health care providers. Such medical expert statements make FMS patients feel neglected, mistrusted, depressed, and without help. Many patients switch to self-blame to intensify the process of pain.

Fibromyalgia's pain and symptoms are real and have a definite physical basis.

Some researchers have speculated that many patients have had FMS syndrome triggered by physical trauma or viral influences. There are no documented anomalies of fibromyalgia patients' muscle tissue, which will account for the illness. Fibromyalgia is not known to cause any illness.

Current research has focused on the brain regions of the FMS patients and the susceptibility to pain sensitivity of certain brain locations. The brain generates a muscle pain warning and stays in an alert condition. The brain does not let go of the pain sensation for unexplained causes, which develops a persistent habit called pain syndrome. The brain stays in a constant feedback loop consisting of an amplified pain-signaling system.

Recent research studies of brain scans have shown a new light on this disorder. Results published in the May 2008 issue of "the Journal of American College of Rheumatology" suggest that neuroscientists have been able to conduct scanning technology to fibromyalgia-affected areas of the brain. In processing the pain sensation, mild pressure on the patient's trigger points has produced measurable brain response. In FMS brain scans, the patient's elevated response to pain was significantly different from those in the study control group. This is one of the research that supports fibromyalgia as a condition impacting the reaction of the brain to the muscle and neuropathic pain. Additional trials would potentially translate into alternative care methods.

Treatment methods generally consist of implementing a multidisciplinary strategy. It is useful for managing medicine, physical therapy, reflection, rehabilitation, alternative therapies, and cognitive-behavioral therapy. CBT is a beneficial medical care choice for pain-stricken patients. The escalation of anxiety and depression can be one of the byproducts of pain. Likewise, anxiety and depression will heighten the pain's effect and make it more painful.

Cognitive-behavioral therapy aims to teach patients with FMS to tolerate discomfort rather than fighting it. Cognitive illusions such as exaggeration and 'catastrophic' need to be addressed for people to understand how to deescalate the stress cycle fueling. How one thinks of one's pain determines its effects. One might learn to respond to pain rationally by saying:

- "I should learn to handle this problem though it's challenging."
- "What is the use of getting upset about my suffering, that's not going to help anyway?"
- "When I move in agony and relax, maybe all of this will become less troubled."
- "I'm not alone in this. I have family and friends helping me."
- "I'm not powerless; I have plenty of methods that I can try to minimize my discomfort. Just keep moving!"

Cognitive-behavioral therapy can help patients with fibromyalgia identify stressful triggers that exacerbate pain. This may involve examining family struggles, exploring internal conflicts, and working with core, self-defeating assumptions that affect thinking and behavior. It is beneficial to teach the patient mindfulness meditation as a means of relaxing the sympathetic nervous system.

Using CBT, a therapist can provide structured homework assignments for the fibromyalgia patient that will help pain sufferers experiment with new behaviors such as increased involvement and activities. This will be beneficial to encourage the customer to establish reasonable targets for day to day working. This is important to promote a multidisciplinary approach that includes exercise, physical therapy, recovery, and pain management.

Patients suffering from fibromyalgia worry that their condition may cause them to lose their capacity to operate at homeland work. It is necessary to encourage patients to focus on what they can achieve rather than their limits. There is a propensity for people with fibromyalgia to interpret truth by focusing on negative thoughts to remove the good. Help to recognize physical disabilities for the individual and families is a critical aspect of effective diagnosis.

Patients of fibromyalgia will quickly get stuck in a pain loop and related depressive symptoms. The goal of Cognitive-behavioral therapy is to help the patient come to terms with their disorder and make plans to manage it. This is accomplished by accepting and teaching the patient, positive ways to think about their condition, and various ways to treat it.

Cognitive-Behavioral Therapy on the Internet Can Benefit Patients with Pain

Cognitive-behavioral therapy (CBT) has shown remarkable effectiveness in helping patients improve their lives with a variety of physical and mental health conditions in study after study. Its use by patients with chronic pain may lead to decreased impairment, decreased depression and anxiety, improved life quality, and even decreased pain.

For those with chronic pain, cognitive-behavioral therapy may be so successful because it works on the convergence between thought and action. By engaging in CBT sessions and doing research, people learn how to identify unconscious patterns of thought that could contribute to harmful behaviors. For instance, patients with chronic pain sometimes avoid exercise as they think it will make their pain worse, and they are more sedentary, and as a result, the pain, as well as general health, worsens.

A short-course treatment typically lasts from six weeks and half a year; CBT equips people with the potential to disrupt and override unconscious thought habits with more realistic and positive behaviors. That, in particular, will contribute to better mental well-being, which in effect, will bring physical benefits as the body and mind's well-being are intertwined. More physical gains, such as exercise, can result from more proactive behaviors.

When a doctor recommends you, certain health care policies will pay the expense of Cognitive-behavioral Therapy, in full or in part. Though a short-course procedure, it may be costly to pay out of pocket. Those who can't access CBT in-person, for whatever reason, may be able to get the same benefits from an internet therapy program.

Internet-Based Cognitive-Behavioral Therapy

A meta-analysis that gathered findings for patients with a variety of physical health conditions from multiple studies on internet-based CBT found it promising to enhance both mental and physical health. They noted that programs tailored to the specific condition of the individual would probably be the most effective. Improvements in physical health were usually more noticeable than in psychiatric situations, with better effects on depression resulting after more than six weeks of care.

Natural Migraine Remedies—Try Cognitive-Behavioral Therapy for Migraines & Give the Pills a Break

Symptoms that let migraine sufferers know the migraine is coming are called prodromal symptoms. Not all migraineurs are lucky to encounter this, but it is appropriate for those who do have the alert; they get to prepare how they will navigate the interruption they are about to join. Cognitive-behavioral therapy may support a migraineur use the same prodromal signs in the migraine assault short circuit.

The goal of Cognitive-behavioral therapy is to recognize and consciously manipulate migraineurs' behaviors that play a role in their headache development. Together, the patient and therapist determine how the migraineur conducts when they feel a headache coming on or when the pain starts for those who do not experience prodromal symptoms. They then try to develop alternative behaviors together to use them in the same situation, which will change the migraine.

In cognitive-behavioral therapy, the therapist and the migraineur work together to:

- Identify the behavior of the problem which needs modification. This is often achieved by keeping a diary about a headache.
- Set a target for the care. At first, it is probably not very practical to aim for total migraine annihilation. Instead, steps should be established along the way, like learning to relax around potential migraine triggers.
- Create new behavior patterns to effect modifications.
- Monitor the patient's reaction to their new behavior as well as check for external factors that may be influencing or affecting that behavior.

Below are some of the more common therapy techniques listed:

- Desensitization
- Positive feelings
- Reframe
- Roll play
- Communicate with yourself

Although cognitive-behavioral therapy is effective in its own right, it is particularly beneficial for patients who already receive therapeutic opioid therapies. A 1989 research showed the effective rate of clinic-based and minimal-touch therapeutic counseling; They had almost the same success rate. This gives migraineurs effective natural treatment.

Education in Cognitive-Behavioral Therapy

Cognitive-behavioral therapy is probably the most widely studied psychotherapy in the country, and it can be learned continuously over a 6-month or 2-year training program, in some instances. Many students who attended a cognitive-behavioral therapy training course reported high teaching success rates and continued utilization of CBT therapies. It would seem from recent studies that more than 90% of all CBT pupils have at least achieved sufficient skill levels.

Because treatment areas will benefit so many patients in so many different situations—such as self-esteem problems, depression, and marital therapy—such abilities and skilled people will be needed in the future. Particularly now that we're all facing an environment full of uncertainty and anxiety, without any visible indications of it calming down.

There is an increasing need for mental health service providers with the current trend towards managed care, including short-term, evidence-based cognitive-behavioral therapy preparation. There is considerable support for the effectiveness of CBT for a wide range of disorders, and that is why we have seen a significant increase in the amount of psychotherapy research and study conducted in this field. Subsequently, several cognitive-behavioral therapy training programs are now available for mental health professionals, but there is always a need to ascertain whether they are effective. This is so that we can ensure that the resources made available are used ultimately.

To do this, different measurement techniques have been established to test and report the effectiveness of these and any future programs that are being developed to help combat the condition. Another such metric is the real degree of maturity that can be displayed in a course or system by participants. Typically, this therapist competence is inferred from therapy results and outcome studies rather than being assessed directly within the training program for cognitive-behavioral therapy.

For example, in real terms, patient adjustments are the main measuring sticks for monitoring and reporting progress from within each class, though this is inaccurate and inadequate since patient improvement can be related to any number of variables—not all arising from the training course or educator.

However, if the overall effectiveness of the programs is to be determined or measured by demonstrated graduate competency levels, a reasonable definition of competency is certainly to be found. In recent years, a small but ever-growing body of research has been emerging and exploring the application of CBT skills as a direct result of cognitive-behavioral therapy training programs. A large proportion of this research has focused on one or more of the three known competence areas.

Education is designed to bring all candidates to a predefined level of competence, resulting in differing variable levels for each trainee. Hence, these studies do not measure the effect of any standard online or offline training course or program.

Cognitive-Behavioral Therapy to Cure Insomnia Naturally

Insomnia is a condition that causes global stress and depression by inflicting millions every night. Such sleep disturbances normally consist of either having a difficult time getting to sleep or constantly waking up throughout the night. There are numerous remedies available on the market today that aim to kill this complicated disorder when putting into action, but many of them are proved unsuccessful. Many insomniacs are looking for natural cures to deprive themselves of sleep. One such popular natural cure is called cognitive conduct therapy. Let's discuss that in greater detail.

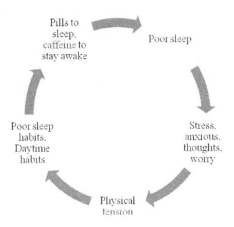

When a person is unable to sleep, this can be the result of many different afflictions. Often, people encounter this kind of sleep disturbance because they face high levels of stress in their daily lives. Insomnia can also arise as a side effect of medication and over-the-counter medicines. Many medical conditions, such as Fibromyalgia, may contribute to sleeplessness. Sleep deprivation disorders may also arise from taking recreational drugs and/or drinking large amounts of alcohol.

Many natural herbal remedies are available to people suffering from insomnia. The use of Melatonin and Valerian Root are some of the most commonly known of these natural cures. When it comes to eradicating insomnia, other forms are considered "normal." Cognitive-behavioral therapy is one of the most popular natural remedies for insomnia and is not medicinal.

Cognitive-behavioral therapy, or CBT, is one of the most effective and newest ways of treating insomnia's disturbing problem. Many people are involved in pursuing this treatment, as it is the best solution to prescribed treatments or medications. It has been known that patients with severe cases of insomnia are often handled for a very long period with prescription medicines. One of CBT's big advantages, though, is that active individuals tend to only use it on a short-term basis to remedy their lack of sleep.

Cognitive-behavioral therapy works on the premise that you are exactly who you think you are. You are doing the acts just as you think you will. The subconscious is the one power that must be changed before any other adjustments can take place. This type of therapy has to be performed by a licensed professional body to naturally cure your insomnia. This practitioner would implement a set amount of sessions to improve the whole thinking process of the individual suffering from insomnia.

First, the specialist must collaborate with the person who cannot properly rest to build a tailor-made plan tailored to the client. Next, the individual is told about the minimum amount of sleep needed to stay safe. During the first few training sessions, numerous ideas and theories will be discussed. An individual will be expected from here to participate in exercises and sessions on preparation. These training sessions are relatively low effort and do not imply any physical endurance requirement. Rather, they will involve a session of "mental reprogramming" of the way the person thinks about sleep.

Throughout the length of these reprogramming sessions, the patient will be told about the behavior they are required to take so that their insomnia can be healed naturally. The directions they receive may consist of waking up every morning at the exact same time and going to bed every night at the same time— this is all part of the reprogramming. Furthermore, the adult can also be instructed to get a certain amount of daylight per day, avoid naps, and even indulge in physical activity for intermittent periods.

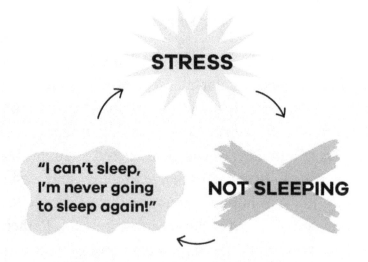

Experts believe the use of cognitive-behavioral therapy to cure insomnia-related problems naturally is extremely productive and successful. Once an individual has completed a set amount of treatments, it is assumed that their views would change in such a way as to spontaneously cure insomnia. Experts agree that cognitive-behavioral therapy may be the best and most successful solution to prescription drugs if you or someone you meet struggles from the stressful condition of restless nights.

Cognitive-Behavioral Therapy—Effective for Eating Disorder Treatment

Health and weight problems are so far more than calories. We derive from psychological problems of many types. Eating disorders may indeed have life-threatening consequences, both physically and emotionally. Currently, if we research the current scenario closely, we can see that eating disorders like compulsive eating or binge eating, anorexia, and bulimia have impacted millions of people in every way of life. Many kinds of mental illnesses and addiction conditions have influenced a number of individuals across the world.

Every year thousands of individuals suffer from eating disorders induced by health complications. Many sufferers rarely receive medication for eating disorders, and those who attempt to manage eating disorders typically adopt treatments such as exercise, fasting, over-exercising, laxative, or use clear tablets. Both approaches can provide influence in the near term, but they do not offer a solution to eating disorders and can also make matters worse. Nevertheless, patients can get well with the right type of eating disorder treatment and eventually learn to eat regularly again. Cognitive-behavioral counseling is also one of the few recovery methods that adopt a psychotherapeutic method that seeks to regulate unhealthy thoughts, attitudes in a goal-oriented structured process.

Cognitive-behavioral therapy is a type of psychotherapy that usually emphasizes the vital role of thinking about what we are doing and how we feel. This is focused largely on the belief that our emotions are influencing our perceptions and behaviors. Focusing on this prime reality, clinicians seek to help individuals re-form their attitudes around diets and bodies so that they make healthier decisions rather than disordered ones. When clinicians adopt a psychotherapeutic method, they seek to understand by doing what their clients desire. During this treatment procedure for an eating disorder, the therapist's is role is to listen, educate, and encourage, while the client's role is to convey, learn, and execute that learning.

It is important to understand the eating disorder is not necessarily synonymous with food or eating habits. It is linked to many other factors, including societal, family, or psychological issues—and all these factors are affected by cognitive-behavioral therapy. Many people from all over the world who, through this behavioral therapy, have effectively recovered from eating disorders state that their sessions actually helped them to handle their emotions. They developed a healthy eating mindset and strengthened their self-esteem. They learned how to eradicate pessimistic thinking patterns and turn them into a voice of optimism.

It has achieved broad awareness among clinicians and customers alike today. To make cognitive-behavioral therapy more effective, however, be sure to work towards common goals together with your counselor. It's almost like an aggressive therapy form.

Trauma-focused cognitive-behavioral therapy, or TF-CBT, is a technique based on short-term research that is highly effective for trauma survivors in children and adolescents. Trauma is characterized in terms of sexual assault, physical abuse, abandonment, experiencing domestic violence, and experiencing murder or death. Such events may also lead a person to suffer post-traumatic stress disorder or PTSD. The symptoms of this disorder include hyper-vigilance, increased surprise response, avoidance around any thoughts or feelings associated with the traumatic event, nightmares, dreams, or feelings that the event occurs again as well as problems of acting out of behavior. TF-

CBT is based on interventions with cognitive-behavioral therapy and can help an individual regain control over their life.

It takes around 13–18 weeks for TF-CBT to be completed. This starts out with psych education. The therapist helps clients and families understand that their feelings are natural and can be resolved. The therapist teaches the client and family coping techniques such as mindfulness, recognition and comprehension of emotions, and the relation between thinking, feelings, and behaviors, in the next few stages. Parents or guardians are encouraged to learn the plan's phases and highlight the family's importance in the treatment.

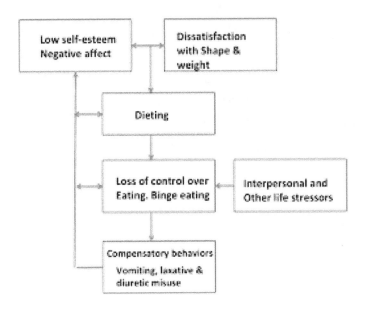

Once these principles have been learned, then the kid tells the story of the experience they have had. The story can be told over multiple sessions, depending on how the client handles this aspect of the treatment. During this phase, it is the job of the therapist to guide and pace the kid in a secure manner through the process. At first, this may sound scary, but the idea is for an individual to become desensitized to the traumatic event by telling it over time repeatedly. The repetition in TF-CBT allows the kid to gain acceptance regarding what happened to them. The client discusses it with the parent or guardian after finishing the story.

TF-CBT's last step is to restructure any of the ideas that pop up in the storytelling that may be contradictory or unhelpful. A common unhelpful thought that may arise, for instance, is, "It was my fault that this happened." The therapist will then help the kid realize that this is irrational by using CBT techniques. It's also essential to address safety during this period. The kid, parent, and therapist can work together to find ways of helping the kid keep safe in the future.

TF-CBT can also be used with children and adolescents who experience other psychological problems such as obsessive-compulsive disorder, separation anxiety, grief, etc.

Chapter 6: Weight Management Using Cognitive-Behavioral Therapy

All too often, diets tend to fail. People set lofty, non-follow-through exercise goals because it's easier not to. With a traditional diet and exercise program, there are so many things that go wrong that it's no wonder why more people are looking for better ways to lose weight and get healthy once and for all. The need to change the whole person versus traditional diets and exercise routines has always been recognized by psychologists. Cognitive-behavioral therapy (CBT) is one method where the clinicians work with people who need to shed excess weight to adopt a healthy lifestyle and create a change from the inside out.

The link between mind, body, and weight management is a lot stronger than many people realize. Dieting and exercising only go as far as the mentality of a human requires. Anyone without determination and pushing through will not see as much gain out of a weight loss program as someone motivated. Using cognitive-behavioral therapy works first to change the thinking, and then the physical appearance will change as the mindset has changed. Therapists are able to help people lose weight, get healthy, and maintain that healthy lifestyle into the future by essentially reprogramming and retraining the mind-body connection.

Yo-yo diets are a prime example of what happens as you try to change the body by altering the mind. When people decide to change what they eat, they often do quite well for a short period. However, eventually, their old habits take hold, and the weight returns because the diet has not changed their mindset at all. People who succeed in obesity management and weight management have been shown to be the ones who undergo therapy or some form of counseling at the same time to get their mind in the right place while also working on their body. When diets, exercise, medication, or even surgery are not enough to keep people thin and healthy, CBT can add that extra push to help give people the lifestyle they always needed.

Getting a clear interaction with a doctor will also build a good link between mind and body through weight loss and make individuals achieve positive outcomes as they have a strategy for themselves. People will learn to improve the way they behave through activities like CBT, yoga, and self-monitoring, which also helps them to adjust the way they cook, workout, and conduct their lives. The goal is the same across the board: To create a healthy lifestyle and to change a whole person so that the health is both physical and mental, instead of focusing on the physical by itself.

The reason diets often don't work and exercise routines are always 'good ideas' and a little more is because people trying to lose weight have unchanged habits and mindsets. Once the entire individual is treated and a brand new healthier lifestyle is developed for the mind and body, weight reduction can be temporary, at best.

Care of Psychological Phobia-Cognitive-Behavioral Counseling—Stoicism and Medicine

First of all, social anxiety disorder or social phobia is the fear of being around other people, or at least the feeling of discomfort. In the broadest meaning, that is the definition of the disease. There are also more common phobias linked to social anxiety disorder (S.A.D.), but our focus with this essay is to look at the numerous therapies available that are appropriate.

The first solution is psychotherapy, and cognitive-behavioral therapy is the first approach to that area. I know we've addressed this before, but I want to come up with it from a completely new perspective and clarify why it's so successful and easier than other types of counseling in producing results. There are 2 main reasons for this.

First, when the psychiatrist and the patient first meet, they arrive at a joint decision on how long the treatment will last. So, they set a target right away. It has been discovered that the average number of CBT sessions a patient has is 16.

Second, compare that with psychoanalysis that can take years.

CBT, on the other hand, is a fairly intense and instructive program and relies on homework in no small part. To prove properly successful, the patient must do their part in the therapy. Assuming the sessions are weekly, the patient then has certain exercises to do at the end of each session to prepare for the next session. Therefore, the course of treatment is not open-ended, unlike so many other forms of therapy.

Third, some practitioners go along with the old stoic treatment line. This basically states that you have one problem if you have one. Then you start to think and get upset about this problem. Now, you've got two issues. The key is to only politely agree and sort things out. Don't worry about it; just sit around. Say it. Do something. Fretting does little but drive yourself deeper and deeper into a pit through which there will be little exit finally.

The first thing a psychotherapist should do is assure the patient that their willpower has no chance of recovering from S.A.D. or any anxiety-based condition. How many occasions we've heard, "Yeah, come on, spit it out." Or, "Suck it up. We all have issues." Patients will be disenchanted with this mindset right from the word 'go.'

I know I've said in the past that I'm no drug lover. It is also completely uncertain what such medications can do to you in the long run. This is particularly true, given that various medications fit different individuals. It's not a case of 'one size fits all.' That being said, if an individual is severely depressed, even near to suicide, that's their state of mind, then some sort of medication needs to be given to relax them.

Anxiolytics, Beta-blockers, and Antidepressants are the three main types. Anxiolytics come in Alprazolam formulations, known as Xanax. Clonazepam, or Klonopin, and Valium or Diazepam. Could we name antidepressants next? These come in Sertraline forms, which is Zoloft. The name for Cymbalta is bupropion, which is Wellbutrin and Duloxetine.

The third type of beta-blockers was used mainly in cases of heart arrhythmias and hypertension. However, in the diagnosis of anxiety problems, other forms have proven very useful. First among them is the Propranolol, invented in the late '50s by Sir James Black. Esmolol, Atenolol, and Acebutolol are other examples of Beta-blockers.

I know I said it before, but it's not enough to say, what works for one person does not automatically work for another. Make sure both of you that the drugs they prescribe are in agreement with your doctor's help. Some people go on drugs for months; that doesn't do the slightest bit of good to them, indeed, often just the opposite, just because the doctor thought it might help. He or she needs patient guidance. If the drug is not working, then find one that suits you.

Seven Pearls for Cognitive-Behavioral Therapy

Research has proven that we can have better control of emotions by recognizing our skewed thoughts and beliefs, and thus better control of our feelings. Having distorted thoughts or beliefs doesn't mean anything is wrong with us. During various points in our lives, we've all had skewed feelings and beliefs. Few descriptions of the misconceptions:

Over Generalizing: We may sometimes see situations as anything-or-nothing. For e.g., if there's one thing going wrong with a project, we may assume the whole project is a disaster. And, if there's one aspect that upsets us about a person, then we might agree that we don't care about that individual.

Mind Reading: We're assuming we know what people are doing. We might say to ourselves that somebody thinks we're "stupid" or doesn't like us even though there's no evidence to support that thought. This is known as interpreting the mind.

Catastrophizing: We overstate how "awful" something is or envision the worst outcome possible. Perhaps our manager wants to talk to us, and we're devastatingly saying that we're going to get fired. And, one day of a break, it floods, and we say, "this is the worst thing that might have happened."

Fortune Telling: We think we know what will happen for sure. We say, for example, "I know I won't get that promotion" or "I'm not going to be able to fulfill the task."

Similar habits or abilities that are often learned include cognitive-communication, assertiveness, interpersonal skills, and strategies for relaxing. Those are taught between and during sessions.

Below, there are seven pearls I would share with you that I consider beneficial in my work over the years:

Train Targets Address

Collaborating on treatment goals is critical during the initial assessment phase. It aids in maintaining the therapy centered and successful. Without expectations, counseling will wind up dwelling on any topic the week pops up and can conflict with the advancement of the initial concerns. The individual cannot be willing to define a target clearly but for a generic, "I want to feel less nervous" or "I want to be happy." In the beginning, everything is good. You should, however, return to this discussion of goals over the first few months to see if they can be described in more specific terms.

For example, if someone has depression, the goals may include: Finding a more fulfilling job, going back to college, exercising three times a week, making two new friends, and stopping marijuana use.

With Agenda off Every Session

Every session will begin with an agenda that is explored in partnership with the therapist and the patient. This helps keep the session focused and more effective once again. The agenda will involve a follow-up of the previous session's assignments, a mood and week check-in, bridging or updating the previous session's issues and development, and subjects relevant to a common objective being addressed at the present session.

Discuss Where to Bring up the Problem

Some expectations for treatment may involve several elements like warped perceptions, values, or habits. Thus, throughout the workshop, the decision is taken collaboratively about the basis to discuss the objectives. If you're focusing on negative emotions, it's crucial to consider what feelings or perceptions happen that contribute to depression, such as fear, depressed mood, or suppressing any behavior. When you're focusing on other things like coping skills or partnership problems, it's important to determine which skills should be needed and how probable those skills are to be used. Another helpful method for solving behaviors is role-playing. It is important to keep visualizing which skill helps improve the behavior and overcome any problems or anxieties about that behavior.

Flashcards US

Flashcards can be used to recall the session's key points or a mantra that may assist with some thoughts or feelings. When I deal with a counselor who is struggling with depression, I would call the flashcard something like a "Survival Kit," and it will include strategies to cope with the stress such as reaching out to a friend, going out of the house, calling out to me or taking care of a minor job.

Based Tell

Goals for rehabilitation are addressed at the start of treatment. Occasionally, the therapy session can go on a path contrary to any of the treatment goals. On many occasions, that is necessary, but if that occurs every session and for the whole duration, then counseling improvement can be minimal. In CBT, the structure is essential, but versatility is necessary as well. This will be an opportunity to meet together and decide whether to stick with the new distraction or the topic being debated or to move to what was addressed in the agenda.

Homework Insign

A collaborative discussion about homework or "action tasks" to be performed between sessions takes place towards the end of each session. An action activity may be to buy a planner where one of the problems is time control or capturing thoughts and photographs that appear in a diary through difficult moments to explore and resolve at the next session. Often make sure that the assignment or action plan is taken up at the next session; otherwise, it gives the illusion that focusing on priorities in sessions is not a vital aspect of getting stronger.

Land for Reviews

Ask what went right throughout the session at the end of the week, what should have gone well, and what the key take-away messages are. This will help develop the relationship, improve potential sessions, and accelerate development.

Cognitive-behavioral therapy is an extremely effective form of therapy with or without medication and is a great way to practice psychiatry.

Chapter 7: Cognitive-Behavioral Therapy in the Treatment of Sex Addiction

"Men are disturbed not by things that happen, but by their opinion of the things that happen." Epictetus.

The psychological foundation for cognitive therapy dates back to the Stoic Thinkers who explained that our suffering is not triggered by the actual incident, but instead by our experience or understanding of the distressing event. According to the Stoics, by changing the thoughts which underlie the distress, people are able to consider alternative perceptions or interpretations.

In the early 1960s, cognitive models became popular. This school's supporters believe that the client's issues arise on two occasions. The first of these is the overt difficulty, like depression or sex addiction. The second involves addressing underlying psychological mechanisms and cognitive psychological distortions, usually involving irrational beliefs that cause addictive behaviors.

Cognitive-behavioral interventions conceptualize developmental issues mainly with respect to ill-healthy behavior, which is geared towards making the person develop more adaptive thinking and behaving ways. This strategy usually relies on instruction, realistic, task-oriented, and instructional approaches.

It's necessary to consider the central concept of cognitive therapy approaches: The apparent condition (sex addiction) originates in what cognitive behaviorists term the schemas of the individual. This is the world view or core belief structure of an individual. This approach focuses on how the client maintains painful, harmful, or irrational behaviors. The primary method allows the use of a sort of debate. This involves pointing out to clients the irrationality of certain thoughts, beliefs, and perceptions and constructing and rehearsing rational self-statements or other cognitive strategies and skills that are more functional.

The emphasis while interacting with a cognitive layout includes:

- The emphasis is on preventing unwanted sexual behavior. To support people to promote abstinence, behavioral intervention strategies (Relapse Avoidance Skills) and/or pharmacotherapy are used.
- This is the "admission" step, which allows the counselor to acknowledge the presence of an issue, which allows the doctor to hold no secrets.
- At this stage, stress management techniques are taught to patients, so they no longer need to rely on sexual behavior to alleviate their anxiety. I recommend physical exercise and teach a combination of breathing techniques, progressive relaxation, meditation, and hypnosis to show clients that they have some power over their inner condition.
- This may be the program's most important stage. It consists of cognitive counseling aimed at repudiating the unfounded assumptions underlying sexual abuse by

constructive interrogation. It helps clients to build a consciousness of beliefs. Clients gain an understanding of their reasoning process by answering questions about how they affect their attitudes and behavior. The client becomes conscious of inappropriate beliefs and is helped to challenge them and change their behavior. The method involves asking questions regarding possible alternative theories that support or refute the feeling. Speaking about the range of consequences of the thought, and how it affects the person, and what the results of accepting the thoughts that modify their mind would be.

- To promote successful social processing, patients are educated in such techniques as assertiveness and problem-solving.
- The emphasis is on fixing any difficulties the person has faced in developing and sustaining a primarily sexual relationship.
- Understanding through thinking patterns contributes to "setting yourself up" for a relapse return.
- Developing a good outlook about safe sex, fostering respect towards one's partners' needs, developing enjoyment skills, use intercourse counseling if sexual dissatisfaction is present.
- Generating pleasurable, happy partnerships and experiences—building a life worth living.

The sex addict relies on sex in order to satisfy their emotional needs, which they cannot achieve by healthy coping skills. Sex becomes a means of coping with stress, shame, guilt, and isolation. It is a way of connecting without placing trust in danger.

The compulsion is never fulfilled, though, as sex cannot satisfy such needs because its root is ancient and the desire is so strong. What's more, sexual activity can never meet the needs of the true self.

Patrick Carnes points out implicit cultural patterns that can be rejected by all sex offenders:

- I'm essentially cruel, an indignant guy.
- Nobody supports me the way I am.
- If I have to depend on someone, then my needs will never be fulfilled.
- Sex is my main desire.

Although these are the central unhealthy values, the addiction process is sustained by even other views, behaviors, or "cognitive structure." Any of them come from experience:

- I can't tolerate boredom; acting out sexually is a good way to fill the time.
- I am overwhelmed with an all-encompassing feeling of loneliness while not disturbed by someone.
- Men have a greater sex drive than women. I need to discharge the drive like a guy, or I'm going to go crazy.
- My self-sense is determined by how many people I get attracted to.
- Life's vicissitudes are dull, even unmanageable. Except for my "closed" universe, there's no fun to have in everyday life.
- Sex with my spouse is a mechanical process that is deadening and loses spontaneity and excitation.

- Life does not offer fun and high-stimulation, so I will forever be lonely and sad.
- I have to succumb to that urge when I get an impulse to act out sexually.
- To be a real male/female, I have to have sex with as many people as I may. Additionally, I am liable, as the one for the enjoyment of my partner by intercourse.
- Intercourse failure is a men-made failure.
- Cybersex involvement is my only means of moving away from the tension and disappointment of life.
- Sexuality is the only trusted means by which to relate to others.
- I focus on sex to fulfill emotional needs, which I cannot reach by safe coping skills.

Addiction is self-perpetuating; it feeds on itself due to ingrained core beliefs as well as the dysfunctional beliefs about sex held by each individual. To reverse the course of addictions, one needs to alter the value structures behind it.

Rationalization, minimization, and reasoning derive from distorted views. If the illness advances, the abuser continues to view the environment through visual hallucinations intended to keep themselves from behaving sexually. Their entire perspective gets distorted to the point where they become ever more out of touch with reality.

Changing those beliefs is key to treatment. Changing core beliefs is a challenge as they have been imprinted at an early age and have been stable over time. Another complicated explanation for reform is that such creeds exist in the unconscious spirit. The addict lacks awareness about their self-defeating convictions. How do you change anything that you don't even know you have? The cognitive trainer elicits these behaviors and values and provides different perceiving and thinking methods.

I sometimes use hypnosis to gain access to the subconscious mind where the convictions, attitudes, and cognitive schemes can be brought to consciousness and disputed.

Treating Tinnitus Noise with Cognitive-Behavioral Therapy

There are different ways to treat tinnitus noise and to relieve patients from the suffering incurred by the ringing noise they hear all day long.

One such treatment is cognitive-behavioral therapy or counseling, which is found to be very effective in treating tinnitus noise by most patients and doctors. It is a general term utilized for a group of similar therapies. There are numerous forms of cognitive-behavior counseling, including logical-behavioral therapy, cognitive therapy, logical-emotional-behavioral therapy, dialectical-behavioral therapy, and cognitive therapy.

Cognitive-Behavior Therapy or counseling

Cognitive-behavioral therapy is based upon the patient's emotional reaction during care initiation. This method of therapy is focused on what psychologists think, that our emotions are influencing our perceptions and actions, rather than actual factors like circumstances, individuals, and incidents.

With that in mind, we should turn our feelings into something that might make us feel better even if we are still in the same position.

Cognitive-behavioral therapy or counseling is suitable for patients with tinnitus activity because the treatment is done for a brief and usually limited period of time. Contrary to psychoanalysis—which usually takes years to get outcomes from—successful results can be observed in no time. Patients are informed beforehand that the therapy will stop, and both the therapist and the client discuss how long the process will take.

A good relationship between the two is also ensured in order for the medication to effectively take effect. Therapists believe that having a positive and successful relationship with their patients is very necessary for them, but they still firmly believe that the latter gets better as they learn to think about different perspectives and work on what they have experienced. In brief, cognitive-behavioral therapy or counseling focuses on the self-consultation capabilities of the participants.

The patients' expectations are very relevant, and clinicians help their clients achieve their goals. The therapist's job is to listen, inspire, and educate their patients, whose function is to understand, communicate their thoughts, and bring into action what they have learned.

Tinnitus activity may be handled as both the doctor and the patient try to accomplish their aims by removing the irritating and distracting ringing noises that the individual experiences. Therapists perceive their customers by the Socrates approach, and that is why they often pose questions. Patients are also encouraged to ask the answers to questions.

Cognitive-behavioral therapy or psychology involves different goals in every course, where the participants are given particular strategies and principles. Clients are the people that state their expectations, and therapists are there just to help them reach them. All contained in the treatment is directed accordingly to the client's desires and making them understand how to behave, function, and achieve what they've always desired (in this situation, to achieve rid of their tinnitus noise. It's not just about what to do; it's about how to do stuff.

Tinnitus Control is an all-natural homeopathic solution for patients suffering from tinnitus. Tinnitus Control relieves tinnitus symptoms and helps stop the constant ringing in the ears.

Treatment of ADD and ADHD—How and when Cognitive-Behavioral Therapy Is Helpful

Students with ADD and ADHD frequently feel that the environment is against them. Their parents show anger and resentment over their bad grades, loss of self-control, and unpaid tasks. Their instructors are continually nagging them about their missed assignments, interruptions, and impulsive responses at recess.

According to the website of the "National Association of Cognitive-Behavioral Practitioners," 'cognitive-behavioral counseling or CBT is an ADD, and ADHD approach focused on the premise that our emotions affect our attitudes and habits, not external factors like objects, circumstances, and incidents.' Hopefully, individuals will adjust their way of thinking and behaving, and therefore, enhance their attitude or responses to a circumstance.

Cognitive-behavioral therapy offers two key approaches to treat adults with attention deficit and hyperactivity disorder:

Tackling Self-Esteem Issues Which Often Accompany Attention Deficit and Hyperactivity Disorder

A 2008 survey conducted in "Infant and Adolescent Psychology and Mental Well-being" found that more than 20 percent of children and teenagers with ADHD were still dealing with mild depression in the research group. Cognitive-behavioral counseling may help children with ADD and ADHD control feelings of inadequacy and open up their outlook about whether people may respond to them in negative ways.

Learning the Ability to Handle ADD and ADHD Symptoms Which Restrict Performance

Cognitive-behavioral therapists listen to the patient's goals and teach them strategies to achieve their goals. Some of the symptoms that are often addressed are anger management, organization, promptness, and commitments. Because it is goal-oriented, the "Mayo Clinic" is considered to be a short-term therapy.

Possible Returns:

- Completing homework tasks during weekly counseling appointments is crucial to meeting goals in a timely manner.
- This approach for ADD and ADHD does not resolve the neurobiological symptoms associated with attention deficit and hyperactivity disorder. However, CBT will not be able to help students with certain conditions, such as the ability to focus more deeply on school work. Thus, Cognitive-behavioral therapy will typically be used in combination with another form of ADD and ADHD care.

Brain Exercise

"Hardy Brain Training" is a game played on the home computer. This ADD and ADHD treatment involve matching simple movements such as toe-tapping with a consistent beat. The goal is to become more accurate each time. As for accuracy, it increases with the game, and so does the efficiency of certain areas of the brain. Once these areas reach a level of efficiency, students start finding learning much easier.

Cognitive-Behavioral Therapy (CBT) and Negative Core Beliefs (NCBs) Identification

Cognitive-behavioral therapy (CBT) is a successful psychotherapy for a wide variety of psychological and emotional disorders. CBT's basic tenet is that our cognitions affect our emotions. To put it another way, it affects the way we think.

A CBT therapist aims to help people with emotional problems by helping them identify the ways their thinking may cause their problems. Therefore, the recognition of "Negative Automatic Thinking" (or "NATs" in short) is the first phase in CBT—these are the feelings that follow uncomfortable or unhelpful emotions such as depression or anxiety.

The CBT therapist's closely related goal is to identify the so-called "Thinking Errors." These are the normal (often unhelpful) ways a person thinks of themselves, others, and the environment around them. These mistakes in thinking will often twist or distort experiences, acting to make the person seem like a failure, others as hostile, and the world as dangerous or disagreeable.

Identifying NATs and associated Thinking Errors is half the battle in CBT—once an individual is conscious of their unhelpful thoughts and mental habits, they may then choose to think more rationally and healthily. A CBT therapist can guide them through that process (fairly straightforward).

I use CBT techniques extensively as a psychiatrist and therapist working in Edinburgh. Some of my clients are quite happy with the results they are receiving by actually questioning their NATs and Thinking Errors—they feel much better and have no need to dig deeper. Most clients, however, are keen to "get to the bottom" of why they first had their emotional problems. I tend to encourage this further research as it tends to validate the progress that has been made so far and, in my opinion, helps prevent the customer from returning at some future date.

This additional work involves looking for "Negative Core Beliefs" (or "NCBs"). These are the unhelpful convictions an individual has had throughout their later childhood and adult life. These are core components of the individual's temperament, and they are the root cause of the person's Thinking Errors, and consequently, their NATs. If a CBT therapist can help a person change their negative core beliefs (or, more realistically, find more rational and healthier alternatives), then the Thinking Errors and NATs of the person will decrease, and their emotional problems (usually!) will decrease.

One difficulty with NCBs is that they are rarely known to a person. Even if someone is able to identify NATs and Thinking Errors, the source of these problems may be hidden away. However, we can use NATs and Thinking Errors as clues.

In my experience as a psychiatrist in Edinburgh, I found the two most advantageous techniques in my clients' search for the NCBs.

Firstly, there is the "Repeated Questioning" process. I'm asking the client what a particular NAT they've identified means to them—they'll give a response, and then I'll ask them what that response means to them. They are going to give a second answer, and then I'm going to ask them what that second answer means to them and so on. The client ends up with a global statement within a short space of time which cannot be taken any further. This is confidence in the "Pessimistic Heart." With one example, it is probably best demonstrated:

Client: "Loads of litter are around Edinburgh" (He's angry)

CBT: "What does that mean?"

Client: "I'm the only one that takes care of it."

CBT therapist: "What does that mean if you're the only one who cares?"

Client: "People don't care about things that don't belong to them."

CBT therapist: "And what does it mean if people care only about their own things?"

Client: "They're just out for themselves"

(This is the "Derogatory Core Belief" of the client—a global assertion that is uncompromising and will clearly influence how they see and communicate with others in many areas of life, not just littering!)

A second way of identifying Negative Core Beliefs is to look for the "themes" that run many NATs and Thinking Errors throughout a person. Such themes may be "I am a failure" or

"There's no point in life" (very common in depression), or maybe "The world's a dangerous place to live" (common in anxiety).

Once the Negative Core Beliefs of a client have been identified, the CBT therapist (along with the client) will attempt to explore alternative and more rational ways of thinking about themselves, others, and the world at large. This is where there is genuine, lasting healing from emotional issues.

Cognitive-Behavioral Therapy (CBT) and Ruminant Depression

Cognitive-behavioral therapy, or CBT, is an effective psychological treatment for a wide range of emotional and psychological issues. As an Edinburgh psychiatrist, I make extensive use of CBT techniques. I also see plenty of depression-stricken people. The emergence of "Depressive Ruminations" is a central aspect of their symptom profile.

The term "rumination" refers to a repeated cycle of activity—this means chewing the cud in the case of cows ("ruminants")! Ruminations are, in CBT terms, the repetitive, almost constant, "stuck" forms of thought found in such psychological circumstances. Depression is particularly common.

The depression treatment goes hand in hand with what you can do for yourself; you need to know exactly what you are coping with before you can treat depression. Depression is no joke because about 15 million individuals suffer from depression in America. The worst thing is that only about 1/3 of those people are looking for support. It is the social prejudices that haunt far too many individuals. Their identity is so vital that they don't want to tarnish it with a word like "nuts." It must first be diagnosed to treat depression. Diagnosis does not arise while the patient is avoiding the issue. It's a vicious circle. This is a vicious circle.

There are many causes of depression. Depression can be triggered by psychological, social, environmental, and physical factors. It is impossible to ignore the genetic link. In many illnesses that are spread along the way, family history plays an important role. Not only the past of the marriage but the family dynamics as well. There's a lot of stress in life. For some, the battle to live week by week is relentless. The question for others can even be performance and transition in culture. Despair can be caused by people who have been physically or mentally exploited. There's no shortlist.

In its early form, depression is often difficult to find. The signs are impossible to see, even if a loved one has this illness. Sadness is part of life occasionally. That is normal. Normally, real depression is much more permanent and more severe. If there are signs of conflict with existence, it is already too late for early detection. Depressed people feel lonely and are dissatisfied with life in general. Throughout their existence, there are no signs of hope. There are no more sleep rituals and life satisfaction. This is when it becomes important to handle it.

A depressed person is supported in various ways by the psychological treatment of depression (psychotherapy). Second, positive therapy helps relieve depressive distress and removes the hopeless emotions that surround depression. Based on the extent of the depression and how many life issues should be overcome, the therapy duration can differ. In many instances, there is an improvement in 6–10 sessions, and in 20–30 sessions, about 70–80% of these therapies are considerably improved. In less time, moderate depression may be treated, and longer therapies may be needed for more severe depression. Treatment sessions normally occur once a week, although they may be originally arranged more often or when a person suffers from serious life crises.

Cognitive therapy removes pessimist thoughts, unreasonable aspirations, and overly negative self-assessments that cause and maintain depression. Cognitive training allows the depressed person to consider serious and trivial problems in life. It also allows them to establish positive life priorities and more positive self-evaluation. Second, problem-solving improves the aspects of the life of the person that cause significant tension and lead to depression. Behavioral therapy can be necessary in order to build better cognitive skills and behavioral care to help solve conflicts in relationships.

Interpersonal (IPT) counseling: Such treatment is short-term and mostly 15–20-session counseling. This lasts roughly an hour for each session. The treatment is primarily concerned with the root cause of depression. It is very helpful for an individual to emerge from traumatic or interpersonal events.

Two different techniques for treating depression include psychodynamic treatment and group therapy. Trauma or disputes are present in infancy, and the treatment takes time, even if deemed short-term. In group therapy, people with similar trauma can interact, and often it is very effective or can share their experience and ways of dealing with it. Nearly two-thirds of the individuals who have been hospitalized have not received proper care.

Depressed patients are considered weak or slow.

Social stigma leads to people being refused the care they seek.

The symptoms are so disabled that the affected persons are unable to find assistance.

Most signs are misdiagnosed as physical issues.

Instead of the underlying cause, specific symptoms are treated.

A psychiatrist will explore the multiple treatment options with you when you have a diagnosis of depression. Illness depends on the type of condition you have. Depression treatment is easier. For starters, antidepressants are recommended for some people with clinical depression. Antidepressants and psychotherapy are also recommended. Other treatments, also referred to as electroshock, may be subjected to electroconvulsive therapy (ECT). This can be used with people who do not respond to standard treatment methods for depression.

For successful depression treatment, the sufferer wants a refreshed sense of hope and purpose. This is often achieved by psychotherapy. After months and years of treatment, it is effective sometimes.

An individual's ruminations can have several "themes," but the most frequent one is a desire for some sort of solution to questions like "Why am I feeling like this?" or "What should I have done to stop that?" Another common theme is one of remorse or regret, "If I had done anything else, I wouldn't be in this position now "or" I ruined my life." There are also pessimistic ruminations regarding the potential. "All is going to go wrong" Ruminations often include what a CBT therapist would call "thinking mistakes."

What does ruminating feel like? Ok, I'm sure we've achieved it all at one time or another! It's like trying to solve an unsolvable riddle-inside your head. You just go round and round, examining the same old 'clues,' time and time again. If you either had this, or mentioned this, or whether you had that, or if you had not. You persuade yourself there is a solution, and you'll be perfect when you discover it. But there is no 'answer' of course. In severe cases, people can ruminate for hours, but up to an hour is more common.

How do you know when you ruminate? Because you stop doing all the rest! For the past 20 minutes, you haven't turned the page of your book, or you're standing in the kitchen with a dishcloth in your hands, looking out into space. If somebody asks you what you thought, you can bet that it's the same old, depressive thought you've been carrying around for ages.

Is there an issue with the ruminating? Well, yeah. It differs in two ways from other forms of thought like problem-solving, reflecting, or remembering. First, most people find this rather disagreeable. The same old concerns are continually churning up to make us feel depressed or nervous. Second, rumination helps aggravate (or at least maintain) stress—if you dwell on how horrible you are and how bleak (you believe) the condition is, then you can neglect the potential for improvement.

Depressive ruminations are seen by CBT theory as a major obstacle to rehabilitation from depression, and as such, clients need to learn how to deal with them. There is a variety of techniques available, but the ones I favor as an Edinburgh CBT therapist are both simple and effective (and almost common sense!).

Now is the time to do something energetic if you realize that you are ruminating. Ruminating is challenging when you are out on a sprint, surfing, or press-ups. The suffering has started to get in the way! Or if you are not the kind that exercises, try to turn your attention to it again. Focus on some aspect of your surroundings—a picture on the wall, a tree, the cat—and examine it for detail, noting every irregularity and color shade.

Pretend you're a famous artist and paint the brightest, most detailed, lifelike picture you've ever seen! Focusing more on issues outside of you (meaning "outside of your head!") helps dislodge your head from ruminative habits. A final tactic—one that some customers swear at and others can't get the hang of at all is to 'stand back' ('in your head' as it were!) and let your thoughts simply churn away while recognizing them as pointless symptoms of your depression. By making them 'get on with it' and failing to 'act' with them, you are disarming them from their depression-causing capacity—they will eventually get bored and quit!

The above techniques are the ones I found working most effectively as a therapist in Edinburgh. There are a variety of other methods in the literature out there, and I'm not saying that this works for everyone. A good thing about the CBT ethic is that it shies away from doctrinal doings—in CBT, there is no "you have to do it like this or otherwise!" So the bottom line is, use whatever method you find that helps you the most, and tell those unpleasant ruminations 'goodbye!'

Causes of Depression

A lot could cause depression. This is generally intellectual, so the main issue is the workings of our brain. Depression may cause behavioral problems, as with many mental disorders.

Depression may arise in factors that cause regrets, guilt, failure, and the like. A person who has failed again and again can lose self-worth and think they are good for nothing. This mentality can deteriorate and lead to depression.

In our brain's functions, genetics also plays a key role. A family with a history of depression can lead to more depression-prone offspring.

Depression signs typically include mood swings and weeping. This disease frequently affects the body. Weight loss, lack of appetite, and insomnia may also be experienced.

Some medications will help reduce depression symptoms. The use of behavioral therapies is a really important thing. These therapies can greatly contribute to tackling the underlying cause of depression.

Therapy sessions can also contribute to improving self-esteem and a better outlook on life.

There may also be the use of antidepressants. These drugs may, however, cause side effects if they are taken regularly. For this reason, many have turned to the natural treatment of depression.

A healthy diet or exercise involves natural cures. The food we eat can sometimes produce happy thoughts. Happy endorphins boost chocolates are known.

Training can greatly help to boost a high level of energy. People are saying that movement creates emotion. This is certainly true but step and enjoy the positive feeling inside you. Staying co-operative and self-lucky does no good for you.

You can also test the marvelous benefits of herbs like St. John's licorice and asparagus roots. It has been found that these herbs are good for reducing depression.

The herbal treatment "Melancholy Lift" can also be sought. This is a great product because the despair and misery induced by stress can be removed. It can contribute to the safe and natural promotion of emotional balance.

The homeopathic ingredients in this drug will assist in a balancing of endorphins that help self-worth and satisfaction.

Homeopathic medicines such as melancholic lift, herbal medicines, exercise, and behavioral therapy are the natural treatment for depression. Furthermore, look for the help of those who love you. It can shift your cynical perspective on life as you surround yourself with people who love you.

Chapter 8: Cognitive-Behavioral therapy (CBT) and Negative Automatic Thoughts (NATs)

Cognitive-behavioral therapy, or CBT, is an effective psychotherapy for many emotional issues. The idea behind CBT is that the way we behave is directly influenced by our emotions—if we act in negative ways, then we feel stressed. As such, a primary goal for a CBT therapist is to help a client recognize when they are unhelpful thinking. This book provides an overview of one way of doing exactly that. I'm going to use the example of someone with social anxiety, a popular issue for people I deal with in Edinburgh as a psychiatrist and therapist.

The first move for the person is to start "recording their feelings" while they feel nervous—that is, writing down what's running through their mind (in short sentences). At first, this may sound a bit odd, but it is really an essential part of the CBT method. Ideally, the clients will pause to write down what they are doing at the time they are talking about it, but it is also appropriate to write it down at the end of the day. They should write down all they thought of—this will generally produce quite a list of thoughts, statements, and beliefs. The client should also note both how they felt (physically and emotionally) and the situation these feelings occurred in.

The client will report, in my case, that the circumstance was a social gathering of colleagues after work. He felt hot and sweaty, his heart was racing, and he was a little light-headed (physical feelings). He described his feelings or emotions as "very anxious." Afterwards, when he returned home, he wrote down the following thoughts he remembered at the time: "I don't know anyone very well," "I have a body odor," "They're all friends," "This place is too busy," "I hate these things," "I want to go home," "I'm going to faint and make myself foolish," "I have to get out of here."

This collection of thoughts he reported is a compilation of what a CBT therapist might call "Inner Depressive Thinking." They are "bad" as they appear to hamper the enthusiasm and ability of the person to engage in activities and add to emotional issues. They're "quick" in that "just like that" seems to arise, bursting into the person's head as if from nowhere. Indeed, unless the person specifically centers his attention on what he feels—as in the practice of the mind—recording-they can go unnoticed. All that the person would then be conscious of is a sudden feeling of anxiety and a desire to leave.

Such negative automatic thinking (or NATs) trigger emotional problems (social anxiety, in this case). Thinking in this way triggers the "fight or flight" response to the perceived threat, leading to physical anxiety symptoms such as heart racing and nausea. If the person didn't have those NATs (i.e., he didn't think things like "I 'm going to faint"), then the response to "Fight-or-Flight" wouldn't kick-in. There would be no physical anxiety signs, and he would be free to enjoy the social doings.

After identifying the client's NATS, the next step is to find alternative, more useful ways to think about the situation. This is better done by considering the validity or "truthfulness" of the NATs; this is done by a CBT therapist (along with the client) by conducting a "trial" for a given NAT. In this case, I will take the NAT "I'm going to faint and make a fool out of myself"—this NAT has been defined as the most distressing thinking by the client (in CBT parlance, this would be called the "Hot Thought").

Evidence "for" and "against" the party concerned is presented in a trial. It is the same in a Negative Automatic Thoughts trial. So what evidence is there that the "I'm going to faint and make a fool out of myself" statement is true? The client felt unpleasant, physically and was anxious. And the evidence to the effect that the thought is false. Much more—he wasn't really fainting, he's never really fainted in all the times when he was feeling anxious, and it's a well-known fear of people experiencing anxiety that they're going to faint. And besides, there seems little evidence to suggest that his colleagues would've been anything but worried about him, even if he had fainted.

The decision, right? That his NAT "I'm going to faint and make myself a fool" is both irrational and false.

Next, it's time to pinpoint an alternative thought that fits the evidence. How about "My heart is racing, and I'm feeling uncomfortable because I'm depressed, but I'm not going to faint, and my fear is going to pass over time?" This seems to be a more accurate statement of the situation and is clearly less likely to exacerbate the symptoms of his anxiety. Thinking this way will reduce his anxiety and allow him to stay out with his colleagues for longer periods, which in turn will help to reduce his anxiety.

Cognitive-behavioral therapy (CBT) says, "We feel our way of thinking." An important first step in recovery from emotional problems is to learn to identify our irrational thoughts (or "NATs") and challenge them. As an Edinburgh psychiatrist and consultant, I considered this to be an important (and shockingly fast) way to ease some of these stress problems, such as depression and anxiety. But this is just a first step, and most clients will benefit from a more in-depth CBT approach that addresses not only their Negative Automatic Thoughts but also their Negative Core Beliefs.

Shy Bladder Syndrome and CBT

What is Shy Bladder Syndrome?

Shy bladder syndrome is a social phobia that affects millions of people around the globe. Social phobia affects sufferers by causing them to feel particularly anxious when performing a task in front of others, putting them at the center of attention. This makes them vulnerable to scrutiny by the "audience" whose criticism they are genuinely afraid of.

This fear of public performance and scrutiny manifests itself in the public restroom or toilet setting for someone with shy bladder syndrome (or paresis as it's also known). For someone with shy bladder syndrome, the toilet is their 'event,' and at the same time, the crowd is made up of all the other people using the bathroom. As a result of this, the fear and anxiety they experience manifest itself in an inability to urinate with others around, regardless of physical need or urgency.

CBT focuses on how our feelings, behavior, and emotions are affected by cognitions (our thoughts). In short, it's 'groundbreaking' straightforward yet successful in its approach, also alluded to as the 'psychology of common sense.' That's why for so many psychiatrists and clinicians, it has been the 'therapy' of choice.

- Identifying unrealistic thoughts—get the opponent identified
- Write those thoughts down
- Analyze the thinking behind evidence that they are true
- Set targets for tackling the problem
- Dismantle the problem into workable parts
- Go one step at a time, towards the goal

CBT and How Effective to Treat Shy Bladder Syndrome

As a social phobia, shy bladder syndrome is primarily caused by the individual having unrealistic thoughts about what other people are thinking about. Consequently, these thoughts (or cognitions) cause them to become incredibly anxious (feelings), which in turn has the devastating effect that they cannot pee (behave) with others around.

As you can see from the breakdown of the actual CBT process, the main focus is to get the individual to first identify any unrealistic thoughts they may have about their problem (e.g., "I'm not able to pee at this urinal and that guy over there keeps looking at me).

Such thinking would seem like a reasonable thought to have provided the situation (it's not 'normal' to be standing in a urinal and not peeing). The vital part of the thinking, however, is what the individual thinks about whether or not the other guy makes any kind of decision about him ("I know he thinks I'm some kind of weirdo"). Thoughts like these come thick and fast and grow out of control quickly to swamp the individual completely. CBT causes the person to identify their feelings, write down their thoughts (get to know your enemy) and then find evidence. In other words, it would ask this individual to find hard, concrete evidence for "I know what he's thinking about me." The truth is, he cannot learn unless the other guy comes over and asks him that way. He assumes. Once those unrealistic thoughts are identified, written down, and refuted due to lack of evidence, they can be clearly seen for what they are (Unrealistic, not evidence-dependent, and not fact-based). This then helps the person begin to more easily identify certain 'inner' thoughts.

That is one stage in the CBT process. In subsequent posts, I will explain how the setting of targets is so necessary to work towards overcoming shy bladder syndrome.

CBT Is Now Used to Overcome Infertility

Get Pregnant on CBT

Last year 30,000 couples in the UK sought help from the medical profession regarding infertility issues. For some women, the cause is biological/medical, requiring professional medical treatment; for the rest, the problem is often psychological, with the barrier to conception being found primarily to be stress-related, psychological infertility.

Stress and its function in pregnancy are the subjects of substantial ongoing medical research; current data show that the body responds to stress by activating the mechanism of hypothalamic-pituitary adrenaline (HPA). This, in effect, releases a number of neurotransmitters, including the main stress hormone, Cortisol, which is known to affect the delicate balance required to ovulate, fertilize, and implant the fertile sperm in the womb.

Using CBT to resolve multiple stress-related conditions is generally recognized and has been the medication option for the majority. While waiting times for CBT treatment at the NHS in many regions are still prohibitive, they are slowly improving as more and more therapists are being trained. Private care is often accessible and provided through such organizations as the "Priory Hospitals and BUPA."

Medical research has now confirmed the positive expected results achieved when CBT is incorporated into the infertility treatment. They have taken the treatment a step further at a small British complementary health clinic in Southern Spain by carefully combining CBT with hypnotherapy, which is, of course, a highly effective mind-body technique, increasingly accepted by the medical profession.

Initially, they use a very detailed set of screening questionnaires, cleverly designed to quickly guide the psychiatrist to any place of tension; if there may be conscious, unconscious, or unresolved life issues, this material is integrated into the CBT. They implement a hypnosis method that encourages extremely intense and normal stages of relaxation and adds highly focused visualization techniques that remove any residual stress or anxiety completely.

Often, women who have attempted to conceive unsuccessfully will be adamant when told that they are not aware of any stress in their lives, which is often the case at a conscious level, but the treatment identifies the many subconscious blocks that can often interfere with the conception. The therapist and the individual work together in a relaxed, therapeutic environment to introduce permanent, long-term levels of positive attitudes and sensations.

At the center, they have spent three years perfecting their methodology; their point of view on stress and pregnancy is in accordance with many other organizations, in that people who are actively trying to conceive everything in their power to keep their bodies in peak condition, take notice of food, rest, exercise, etc. Add to this, the anxiety that women usually experience trying to get pregnant, and the all too familiar negative loop is gripping. Going through the treatment of infertility and experiencing the invasive nature of the procedure can be extremely stressful, and when this anxiety is added to the negative effect caused by the situation on the relationship of the couple, then stress levels often go through the roof, which dramatically reduces the design changes. Of course, stress can also affect a man's sperm quality and mobility.

In comparison with alternatives, the therapy method used at the clinic is inexpensive, non-invasive, and, many confirm, a surprisingly pleasant experience; clients are predominantly British couples who fly over specifically for treatment for a few days. Additionally, of course, they have the opportunity to spend a couple of quality days together on the Mediterranean coast, enjoying the sunshine in a relaxed environment that can only compliment the therapy and help to achieve the perfect successful recipe.

Treating IBS with CBT and Hypnotherapy

The chronic disease irritable bowel syndrome, known as IBS, currently affects up to 8 million people in the UK, and a clear origin is still not identified by the medical profession. Approximately 50% of the sufferers claim that their symptoms started at a traumatic time of their life, such as divorce, moving home, abrupt work loss, or bereavement. Many people believe that an allergy to specific foods causes their IBS, as eating a meal often causes the symptoms.

Established forms of therapy for IBS involve lifestyle modifications, anti-spasmodic drugs, muscle relaxants, and even anti-depressants, although this has sadly proven unsuccessful for a variety of people.

Recently, the medical community on all sides of the Atlantic has started to prescribe Hypnotherapy or CBT as pioneering therapies after extensive studies into the advantages received by IBS sufferers.

In 1995, a study was completed at "the State University of New York" in Albany on the positive efficacy of using CBT to alleviate the symptoms of IBS: In addition, recent research published in the BMJ concluded that approaches such as hypnotherapy, cognitive-behavioral therapy (CBT) and antidepressant drugs could be of great help.

A clinic in Spain took the treatment with IBS a step further by combining the two therapies, resulting in a much-focused approach.

They spent four years developing their treatment at the small British clinic in Fuengirola, which they successfully utilized on a range of stress-related conditions, including IBS. The therapy is called life architecture(TM) and consists of a range of components, one of which is the intelligent combination of both CBT and hypnotherapy, with one therapy being used to support the other as and when necessary—often producing quite exceptional results.

The treatment contains nothing that's fresh, but its philosophy and technique are definitely different, especially the mixing of therapies. The therapy incorporates the use of its own method of forensic-diagnostic examination, designed to ensure that the psychiatrist has the best chance of finding and addressing the main cause of the problem efficiently, rather than the symptoms.

While the clinic offers its non-residential treatment package to the ever-increasing number of Brits living in Spain, it continues to receive almost daily inquiries from people interested in traveling to Spain for a few days for low-cost treatment, much to everyone's surprise.

CBT's Position in Handling Grief

There's something truly unique about creation. Life is unpredictable, and that's what leads to the excitement and everyday difficulty of meeting it. You have ups and downs, highs and sorrows, happiness and pain, all wrapped into one. For many folks, however, grief is an emotion that they face and deal with problems.

There's a lot of grief that you face when you're losing someone close and dear. Although after a few days of sorrow and grief, a lot of people return to normal, there are some who get into a deep depression because of grief. These people can't cope with the intense sense of loss they can feel. This comes in the way of normal living and regular life, meaning that such people need professional assistance. This professional medical assistance is in the form of CBT or Cognitive Behavior Therapy, which is well acknowledged to be effective in helping grieving people.

CBT practice is based on the understanding that actions and feelings can be modified based on a change in thinking. If the thinking patterns are positive and healthy, you can feel good and demonstrate good behavior. A ton of CBT can be given to the individuals who get into a pit of constant sorrow. CBT helps these people cope with their sadness and developmental energy techniques. This is by gradually replacing sorrowful thoughts with positive thoughts and less melancholic ones.

The use of rationality, in combination with emotional healing, helps patients suffering from acute grief. A qualified CBT counselor can help such patients in trying to understand the root causes of grief. At the same time, patients are taught coping mechanisms by grief counseling so that patients get to cope with the issue well.

Modification of the thinking process is not easy or any quick fix. It can be stretched out long, where the whole cycle of thinking would also need to be changed and uprooted. It requires a lot of patience from the professional CBT specialist as well as patient cooperation. It is this two-way and multi-pronged approach that can deliver the best outcomes in dealing with grief.

Dialectical-Behavioral Treatment (DBT) versus Cognitive-Behavioral Therapy (CBT)

Dialectical-Behavioral therapy (DBT) is a therapeutic methodology developed by Linehan, a researcher from "University of Washington psychology" for treating people with borderline personality disorder (BPD). DBT blends cognitive-behavioral therapy and clinical methods from different practices, including Western mindfulness techniques. Analysis has shown DBT to be the first effective therapy for treating BPD. Further research has been conducted, and it appears to be effective in treating people with a spectrum of mood disorders, including self-harming behavior. After realizing other therapies were ineffectual when used for BPD, Linehan created DBT. She acknowledged that the chronically suicidal people she worked with were brought up in invalidating environments and required unconditional acceptance to develop a successful therapeutic relationship for them. She also argued that people must recognize and accept their low level of emotional functioning and be prepared to change their lives.

For at least two reasons, it is extraordinarily difficult to help the person with borderline personality disorder make therapeutic changes in their lives. First, concentrating on therapeutic improvement, either by encouragement or by teaching new behavioral skills, is often viewed by traumatized individuals as invalidating and can precipitate depression, non-compliance, and exclusion from therapy on the one side, or frustration, hostility, and assault on the other hand. Second, ignoring the patient's need to change (and thus not promoting much-needed change) is also experienced as being invalidating. Such an approach does not take seriously the very real problems and negative effects of the patient's behavior, which, in addition, will precipitate fear, hopelessness, and suicidal ideation.

The Two Components of CBT

1. An individual component in which the therapist and patient discuss issues that arise over the week is recorded on diary cards and follows the target treatment hierarchy. Typically, these sessions last 45–60 minutes and are held weekly. Self-harming and suicidal behaviors take precedence, followed by behaviors that interfere with therapy. Before that, there are issues surrounding life and working quality to improve one's overall well-being. Both the therapist and the patient work towards improving skill utilization to survive and manage difficult feelings during individual therapy. The whole session should be working towards a validating setting for the patient. The immediate concerns, feelings, and actions should be given considerable

attention. A capabilities community is often debated, and obstacles to skillful acting are tackled.

2. The group, which usually meets once a week for two to two-and-a-half hours, learns to use specific skills that can be broken down into four modules: Core mindfulness skills, interpersonal efficiency skills, emotion regulation skills, and distress tolerance skills. The room should be arranged like a classroom with the trainers placed at the front (usually two). Issues and emotions are discussed and dealt with if group therapy is life-threatening or interfering. For example, if somebody behaves badly this would be addressed only if it caused a problem with the group running. Otherwise, it would go overlooked. Skills Training is conducted around a manual which gives details of the program to follow. That provides guidance and advice on how to teach it. It also contains personalized handouts. Group work can involve role-playing, and homework is encouraged as in CBT.

Commitment

The patients have to make a commitment to participate in the therapy before DBT can begin. This is an exercise in itself and may have several meetings to take place. Both the counselor and the psychiatrist participate directly. In reality, the therapist may first 'play hard to obtain' and guide the individual to persuade them that the plan is warranted too.

People with BPD have frequently experienced treatments which were unrewarding at best. The resultant warmth needs to be validated, and the new therapeutic initiative described as exciting but also challenging in a realistic way. Time spent on prior therapy commitment is a good investment. Likewise, if the therapeutic relationship is wobbled or begins to break down, time is needed to maintain that engagement. It's common for there to be an agreement that if for any reason three consecutive sessions of one kind are missed, then the patient is out of the DBT program.

Common Commitments in DBT

Patient Agreements

- Agree upon a particular time limit to stay in a therapy session
- Make emphasis on reducing suicidal thoughts/ behaviors
- Attend all therapy sessions
- Engage in skills training

Therapist Agreements

- Try at all times to conduct competent Therapy
- Always endeavor to be ethical and professional as per professional guidelines
- To maintain confidentiality
- Obtain consent always
- Always make yourself available for therapy sessions and back up when needed

None of these elements are alone in operation. The personal aspect is considered important to avoid suicidal thoughts or unresolved emotional problems from affecting group sessions, whereas group sessions incorporate DBT-specific strategies and can offer opportunities to manage feelings and actions in a social setting.

The Four Modules

Mindfulness

One of the main principles behind DBT is being mindfulness. It's the desire to pay attention to the current moment, in a non-judgmental manner. Mindfulness is about living in the moment, fully experiencing one's feelings and senses, yet with perspective. It is considered a framework for the other skills learned in DBT, as it allows people to recognize and accommodate the strong feelings they may experience while questioning their behaviors or introducing themselves to stressful circumstances. The concept of mindfulness and the meditative exercises used to teach it are derived from traditional Buddhist practice, though there are no religious concepts in the version taught in the DBT.

Interpersonal Effectiveness

Interpersonal response patterns are very similar to those taught in many assertiveness, and interpersonal problem-solving classes taught in DBT skills training. They provide constructive approaches to know what one may like, to learn to say no and to deal with interpersonal confrontation. In a general sense, individuals with a borderline personality disorder often possess good interpersonal skills. The problems arise by adapting certain abilities to a particular situation. When discussing another person facing a problem situation, an individual may be able to describe effective behavioral sequences but may be completely unable to generate or perform a similar behavioral sequence when analyzing his or her own situation. The behavioral element of efficacy focuses on scenarios where the goal is to alter things (e.g., to persuade someone to do something) or to resist changes that someone else is trying to make (e.g., saying no). The techniques learned are intended to increase the likelihood of achieving the needs of an individual in a given circumstance and at the same time avoiding hurting either the partnership or the client's self-respect.

The Regulation of Emotions

Individuals with a borderline personality disorder, and individuals who commit suicide are often emotionally intense and labile. They may be angry, frustrated, discouraged, or nervous. This indicates that these clients may benefit from learning aid in regulating their emotions. Dialectical-behavioral emotion regulation skills include:

- Defining and label out emotions
- Identifying barriers to emotional improvement
- Reducing emotional vulnerability
- Increasing emotional positives
- Acquiring knowledge of existing feelings
- Doing the reverse
- Applying immunity to anxiety

Tolerance of Pain

Many current mental-health treatment approaches focus on changing distressing events and circumstances. They cared little about accepting, finding meaning for, and tolerating distress. Psychodynamic, psychoanalytic, gestalt, or story treatments have typically addressed this mission, along with religious and spiritual cultures and members. Dialectical-behavioral therapy stresses skillfully understanding how to handle the pressure.

Skills in awareness of pain represent a normal evolution from skills in mindfulness. They have to do with the ability to accept both oneself and the present situation in a non-evaluative and non-judgmental way. While this is a non-judgmental stance, it doesn't mean it's one of approval or resignation. The aim is to become able to calmly recognize negative situations and their impact, instead of being overwhelmed or hidden from them. Instead of falling into the intense, desperate, and often destructive emotional reactions that are part of borderline personality disorder, this allows individuals to make wise decisions about whether and how to take action.

Tolerance techniques involve progressive approval, transforming the mind towards tolerance, and discriminating between "will" (skillfully behaving, with a rational view of the present situation) and "must" (trying to force one's irrespective of reality). Participants also learn four crisis survival skills to help deal with immediate, seemingly overwhelming emotional responses: Distracting one-self, self-reassuring, improving momentum, and thinking about the pros and cons.

Cognitive-Behavioral Therapy Reduces Pain, Increases Coping with Rheumatoid Arthritis

According to one major research carried out by Matcham et al. on the incidence of depression in patients with rheumatoid arthritis, approximately one-third of patients are thought to suffer from depression. There are many and varied reasons for this correlation, not just for arthritis patients but more generally for chronic pain patients.

Pain affects life in several respects and produces additional stressors that are hard to deal with. Pain conditions, for example, may interfere with your ability to work, perform the activities you love and even perform basic daily tasks. The need to rely more strongly on others will contribute to feelings of failure and worthlessness. What's more, pain is anxiety-inducing; anxiety over how you'll actually survive will trigger significant concern and depression. Lastly, there is a biochemical linkage between physical pain and depression. Both are stored in the same brain areas, and an increase in activity from stimulation in one can cause an increase in the other's sensation.

Rheumatoid arthritis is a progressive disease, which can lead to disability and joint disfigurement unless the disease progression is disrupted. Medicines are generally relied on to prevent change, but they aren't successful for all and come with serious risks. Patients need to know about all treatment options which have the potential to help them survive with less discomfort and higher life quality. Cognitive-behavioral therapy may be beneficial to patients with this condition, according to recent research.

More generally, Cognitive-behavioral therapy (CBT) has a strong track record of effectiveness for patients with chronic pain. Patients learn how to develop better coping skills in treatment sessions with a therapist. They analyze their thoughts, feelings, and beliefs about pain, seeking to eradicate and replace counterproductive cognitions with more accurate, constructive, and productive ones. This method of therapy has been found to improve not only with mental and psychological functioning but also with pain intensity; this may be attributed to the effect on activity rates with healthy cognitions as well as the physiological relation mentioned above. The research of patients with rheumatoid arthritis showed that those who obtained CBT reported reductions of physical pain and depressive problems that continued up to the follow-up span of 12 months.

Sciatic Nerve Treatments: Cognitive-Behavioral Therapy as an Alternative

Typically, when folks struggle with sciatica's debilitating discomfort, they seek skilled help in the form of CBT or cognitive-behavioral therapy, a branch of psychological therapy. The doctors often urge their patients to gain some mental and emotional control over their pain even before prescribing powerful medication for sciatic nerve treatments. In the case of pain control, therapy is a process that helps patients understand their response to pain and develop certain behavioral triggers to ease the discomfort naturally.

Going to a CBT therapist doesn't mean you could be insane. To be ashamed of or kept hidden from friends and loved ones is really absolutely nothing. On the opposite, CBT is simply a technique in which the psychiatrist proposes ways to change the emotional reaction, actions towards, and thoughts towards the distress you experience as a way of either staying free of or eradicating the internal stress that typically adds to what seems to be constant misery. CBT lets you concentrate exclusively on your sciatica pain and ways of coping with the distress that both decreases it and frees your mind from the unpleasant feelings that typically surround the pain.

Although CBT does not completely relieve you of your suffering, it helps you respond to several of the forces that surround the suffering. Patients going through CBT experience less discomfort, are much less irritable and tend to have a better pain threshold. They also report increased physical activity, improved relationships with their loved ones, colleagues, and pals. These are just a few of the benefits which many men and women report receiving with CBT.

My buddy from "The Internet Depression Recovery Center," Jerry Berger, tells me that one of the causes for moderate or even severe depression is long-term pain suffering. Several folks with sciatic nerve discomfort develop symptoms of depression on top of their sciatic discomfort, especially if their suffering is ongoing and lasting for a long time. It is evident that emotional illness or traumatic situations will bring about certain types of depression, as well as other physical ailments. In short, we get the ability to get sick. CBT's main benefit is that its sole purpose is to concentrate on those mental aspects that are synonymous with pain and usually stop the damage before it begins. CBT is a skill-based therapy that gives you the tools and strategies to tackle your discomfort. In CBT, you learn techniques such as meditation, breathing, muscle relaxation, strategies that address pain tolerance, and solutions that attack discomfort from the beginning as opposed to waiting until it is really in full-on mode.

As an approach to the treatment of sciatic nerves, CBT offers you natural, conservative approaches to addressing discomfort. Additionally, the techniques you acquire in CBT to treat sciatica pain transform into methods that you will be able to utilize in the future to combat fear, stress, or any pain and discomfort instances. This treatment provides you with a completely new collection of instruments; what you have to do is use them.

Cynicism and pessimism are addressed by integrated behavioral therapy.

Disproving or countering negative emotions and thoughts is a process called "cognitive restructuring." Here, a person with an anxiety disorder is helped by refuting pessimistic beliefs and feelings that might lead to a panic attack on them. Negative premises are replaced with more positive and realistic principles, with the assistance of a therapist to help the person overcome anxiety disorder. That will require three stages:

The first stage involves the identification of negative ideas. Anxiety disorder leads people to exaggerate that their conditions are bleak, but in reality, they are not as severe as they seem. Most individuals will understand that the worries are unfounded, even the subjects of an anxiety illness themselves. They are, however, so much crippled by such fear that they can't do anything about it. That makes it difficult to identify negative thoughts, but one method for overcoming this is to ask yourself what you think if you feel anxious. It's also a widely employed technique for therapists.

The second stage involves the testing of negative thoughts. This is where a therapist will assist you in assessing the validity and reason behind negative thinking. This involves verifying evidence, investigating misconceptions, and examining whether negative predictions apply to reality or not. Strategies to do this include testing, evaluating benefits and drawbacks, and discussing odds about what is presently likely to happen and not what you believe will happen.

The third and final stage is more about substituting pessimistic and irrational opinions for optimistic feelings. Here the misrepresentations may be substituted with more accurate and constructive logic until they are established and disproved. A psychiatrist will help you bring out positive words that you should talk to yourself if a person faces difficult situations.

Simple Steps in Which Cognitive Therapy Can Positively Develop Your Self-Esteem

Cognitive implies "thought related" behavior means "how an individual reacts to a particular set of conditions" Let's bring together those two words: Cognitive behavior is then the way we think about our reaction to a set of conditions.

How this contributes to our self-esteem is a vital component of learning how to improve our situational patterns in order to avoid our self-esteem from taking such a hit. Low self-esteem has a detrimental effect on all facets of our lives, in our marriages, in our jobs, or even in our well-being. If we can find a way to stop that kind of self-judgment, it will be easy to lift our self-esteem to a far higher degree, irrespective of how weak our self-esteem is before we continue.

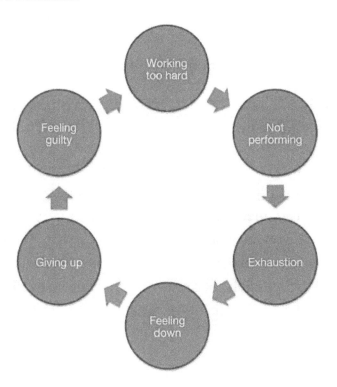

CBT (cognitive-behavioral therapy) helps us adjust our behavior patterns and unhealthy thinking and judgment. The philosophy behind CBT is that our thoughts and feelings about ourselves are determined by what we believe about ourselves and our lives. This method works because it helps us to become conscious of such negative thoughts and feelings, and then we can replace them with much more positive thinking.

Below are CBT's 5 basic steps:

Step 1: Identify Situations that Disturb You or Are Stressful

What brings down your self-esteem? Criticism, right? Ever expect the worst? Do you normally feel angry? Will you feel nervous about conflict or presentation? Will you have some unhealthy practices forever? About food? Expenditure over?

Step 2: When These Situations Occur Evaluate your Thoughts and Beliefs About Yourself

Now it is time to do an honest assessment. Notice your thoughts when it comes to the above situations. Do you start a conversation with yourself immediately in your mind, where you berate yourself that you are not good enough, smart enough, fast enough, or rich enough? Are your thoughts all negative about yourself? Is it possible because of your internalized negative beliefs that you are misinterpreting situations and people's responses to you?

Step 3: Identify Your Possibly Specific Negative Thoughts

You become what you think. If you think you're a dumb idiot, you're likely to strengthen that belief and eventually become inept and incapable of doing anything right. Be careful about this sort of putting yourself down. When it comes to questions about self-esteem, we are often our own worst rivals.

Step 4: Ask the Questions Yourself

You won't be able to do this overnight, but by observing such negative thoughts, you can slow down and ask yourself to answer the question honestly, "Is this really true about me?" You can start to be a little more positive once you begin to notice your negative thoughts. Not all of the bad stuff that you think about yourself is real. Ask yourself, "Did I do anything right or good in this situation?"

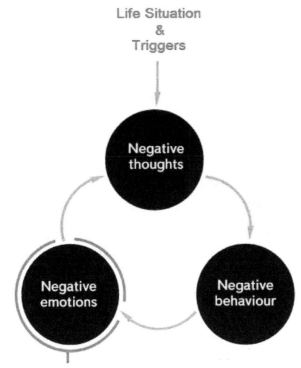

Altering Emotions Through New Thinking & Behaviours

Step 5: Change the Way You Think About Yourself

This step is the most difficult, but you have to do it to change your self-esteem. You need to replace your negative thoughts with more positive thoughts and self-beliefs. Start with just one, and go on. It'll take a little practice, but sometimes it's the only key you need to make a huge change in your life.

Behavior Therapy for Restless Leg Syndrome

While restless legs syndrome is considered a neurological disorder, it is also commonly referred to as a sleep disorder as it primarily affects the ability of the patient to have proper sleep nights. Individuals suffering from extreme symptoms associated with RLS are expected to get just around five hours of sleep a night, which is the least amount of sleep relative to the other forms of sleeping disorders.

Sleep deprivation was correlated with an individual's failure to relax as well as numerous underlying mental illnesses including depression and anxiety disorders; so many patients suffering from restless leg syndrome undergo behavioral therapy medication to solve or remove their RLS symptoms.

Cognitive-behavioral therapy or CBT is used for the treatment of many types of sleeping disorders, including insomnia and restless legs syndrome. There are many different approaches that can be used in CBT to treat sleep disorder symptoms, including stimulus control that has been effective in treating insomnia patients as well as secondary insomnia, such as that caused by RLS symptoms. Stimulus management is focused on improving the actions and thought habits of the individual when it comes to bedside and sleep.

Some sleep precautions are prescribed to the patient, such as using the bed solely for sleeping, setting different hours for going to bed each night as well as getting up in the morning irrespective of how much sleep was achieved. If, within fifteen to twenty minutes of going to bed, the patient is unable to fall asleep, they are encouraged to get up and move to another room or perform any other type of exciting activity, such as reading. Napping can also be stopped because this may greatly mess with one's sleeping capacity at bedtime.

Other Restless Legs Syndrome CBT Methods

Cognitive-behavioral therapy for sleep disturbances often includes altering pessimistic sleep perception habits and replacing them with more optimistic ideas. For example, the patient is encouraged to replace their negative thinking with optimistic affirmations or pictures, including "I will never fall asleep."

Image therapy can also be beneficial for sleep disorders and consists of mental tasks or images given to the patient that can distract them from focusing on their inability to fall asleep, which has been beneficial in allowing many patients to fall asleep more quickly. While behavioral therapy helps numerous people suffering from the condition of restless legs, this method of medication is most successful when paired with improvements in diet and lifestyle, as well as certain types of care recommended by a practitioner.

Conclusion

Cognitive-behavioral therapy is a psychological discipline that aims to help people cope with dysfunctional emotions. Cognitive-behavioral therapy, unlike other types of open-ended therapy, is goal-oriented and systemic. This type of therapy is frequently used to treat mood disorders, anxiety disorders, psychotic disorders, substance abuse, and an eating disorder. Additionally, the therapy has been shown to be effective in treating post-traumatic stress disorder, OCD, depression, and even specific disorders such as bulimia nervosa for some populations.

Due to CBT's efficacy, it's often a very brief experience, unlike some other forms of therapy that can go on for months to end. CBT may be formed independently or within a community. Some modern efforts have been made to use CBT to change the treatment environment for inmates. In such cases, therapists attempt to re-educate criminal offenders on cognitive abilities and coping mechanisms that will help reduce criminal behavior.

Therapists/doctors will be identifying and monitoring the thoughts and beliefs of a patient in that process. (This will be discernible through a series of tests) The objective is to determine how these beliefs relate to weakening behavior, such as alcohol abuse, criminal behavior, etc. In the 1960s, Cognitive-behavioral therapy was created in an effort to combine the best results of behavioral therapy with those of cognitive therapy. While these two disciplines had very different origins, when focusing on treatment, they found common ground.

In this discipline, there are two main components to be analyzed, and these are also the two main theories at work: Cognitive and behavioral. If you have a social anxiety disorder but don't want to explore the medication option, then Cognitive-behavioral therapy is a great alternative. Yes, it is currently considered to be the most effective form of managing social anxiety disorder.

I have been following a progression of fashionable therapies since the late 60s and studying others back to the turn of the preceding century. I saw little new, truly. Mostly merely repackaging under a new authority. Long before the term "CBT" became popularized, psychologists made full use of it, but they just spoke of an "eclectic cognitive restructuring approach" or "behavior modification techniques." Then there is the question of the efficacy of one therapy compared to another. No dearth of impressive-looking work seems to show that every treatment is superior to each other! And note well: CBT is not a single therapy or technique either.

Katy Grazebrook & Anne Garland writes: 'Cognitive and behavioral psychotherapies are a range of therapies based on concepts and principles derived from psychological models of human emotion and behavior, including a wide range of emotional disorder treatment approaches, from structured individual psychotherapy to self-help material.'

Wikipedia Free Dictionary: 'Cognitive therapy or cognitive behavior therapy is a kind of psychotherapy used to treat depression, anxiety disorders, phobias, and other forms of mental disorder. It involves recognizing and reacting to unhelpful patterns of thinking, then modifying or replacing them with more realistic or helpful ones.'

The foregoing "definitions" have the practical advantage that they don't really describe CBT; they don't tell us where it starts and ends. For example, the net effects of quantitative studies comparing CBT with a variety of other therapies were released. One of those other therapies is "modeling" (I name it monkey-see-monkey-do).

If I'm right, and CBT, as it is applied, is a mishmash of therapeutic approaches that have always been used in an eclectic approach to psychotherapy, then one might ask if there was any need to develop the word CBT? Well, for starters, it explains my book, and I think that it helped American psychiatrists market psychotherapy to a relatively new "managed health care" (insurance) program as being "evident."

Cognitive-behavioral therapy (CBT) can be viewed as a repackaging and franchising of a collection of treatments going back to the 1960s, possibly with some focus on Albert Ellis' ('A Roadmap to Moral Living,' Harper, 61) 'Rational Cognitive Therapy' (RET), which incorporates much of the core values of Buddhism (without Nirvana and reincarnation), and Donald Michaelbaum's (1970s) 'self-talking' therapy.

CBT may include Maxwell Maltz's "Psycho-Cybernetics" (like a servo-mechanism, we automatically approach more and more accurate approximations of our persistent goals) and Tom

Harris's "Transactional Analysis" (TA), which is a simple, pragmatic and non-mystical explanation of psychodynamics.

Naturally, the element of "behavior therapy" or "behavior modification" makes use of the concepts of traditional and functional conditioning, i.e., associating one item or action with another, e.g., a reward, or an escape, i.e., reinforcement. To be effective reinforcement, it requires incentive, a need, or a "driving state." Thus, a reaction to the first thing is changed, or a behavioral style becomes adjusted.

In action, the "conduct" component of CBT also includes the use of Wolpe's progressive desensitization technique (or variation) that was originally based on the (partly false) idea that fear cannot occur in the midst of skeletal relief. This method involves a yoga form of progressive relaxation along with graded visualizations of the threatening situation.

The main things: Panic, anxiety, depression, phobias, traumatic and other stress disorders, obsessive behavior, and problems with relationships.

The procedure

A. Define the problem in collaboration with the client if the problem is intermittent, looking for triggering or precipitating factors try to formulate concrete behaviorally observable therapy goals. " How would you show your improved trust to others? "How could your improvement be measured? How do you know you're really "better"?

Help the health center anticipate a favorable result. This utilizes advice. Doctor's words on medical matters have enormous suggestive power, even their frowns, grimaces, and "hmm hmms" and can do both harm and good. Anxious patients are prone to misunderstanding and putting down negative interpretations of what they are told. They may also hear only some keywords and fail to put them in the context of other words that they may not "hear" or understand, i.e., they "look for trouble," jump to the wrong conclusions or use a term coined by Albert Ellis, "catastrophic."

B. Of course, CBT requires all the normal forms of good practice that are best described elsewhere in counseling techniques.

C. Making use of any mixture of the following according to the criteria posed by the client's question and lifestyle:

1. Easy steps, such as steady diaphragmatic breathing during heart attacks, having adequate sleep, and paying attention to a healthy diet and regular social interaction. Mental practice (cognitive): (A) Challenge the client to split a suitable answer into a series of phases or levels. (B) Let the client visualize in reality, executing any desired move leading to a satisfactory answer. (C) Set up a homework task of actually experimenting and practicing in the "real world" some or all of the confidence-building steps.

2. Journal of the Client: A diary may be divided into time slots, if necessary shorter than a day. Or the diary can concentrate on only the significant events. Any headings: (a) the moment, (b) what happened, (c) how I was really acting, including what I did, and (d) what I thought? (E) What should I do next time/will I do? The

diary or journal may be a powerful learning resource for mental training over time and a source of motivation and encouragement.

3. Modeling: This is what I call "monkey see monkey do." By observing and receiving encouragement and useful feedback from someone who is an expert in the desired behavior, it involves learning in its purest form. Practice and know-how banish anxiety. This is how all vital skills from surgery and aviation to panel beating are learned. I once sent a shy youth out in the night club with another young man who was experienced in meeting opposite-sex acquaintances and totally devoid of social fear. Training videos can provide a practical and convenient modeling form. For instance, there was a time when Cerema Clinic from South Australia's "Mental Health Service" used videos to model sexual behavior for sex therapy. Videos on various subjects may be useful to business citizens with performance-related anxieties (e.g., presenting during events or relating to individuals with high rank—executive phobia). Modeling can entail entering a particular interest community for preparation, e.g., "Toastmasters" as part of the reading, or the "Penguins."

4. Relaxation expertise: This may involve widely employed hypnotherapy methods. The calming technique strongly fits the style of soothing yoga. Once a pleasant state of relaxation or trance is achieved, it is possible to attempt systematic desensitization, and thus, methods such as encouraging clients to build their own mental place of refuge to which they can retreat whenever they choose for mental refreshment —it can be just a room or a castle or whatever the client likes. The invention by a

client of a fictitious guru or teacher may be a variation or addition to this technique. Some religious people already use that technique as a belief in guardian angels. Yet, there is no requirement for absolute conviction.

5. Systemic desensitization: e.g., with a phobia spider. The patient is guided through a relaxation routine similar or identical to the yoga exercise, and maybe then ask to visualize a small spider at the end of a long hall—so far away it is difficult to see. When the patient is able to visualize this without increasing tension (the patient can indicate tension by raising the index finger), the image becomes slightly more dangerous. For spider phobias, I make use of a children's book with the artists' welcoming, stylized, beautiful spiders kept at a stand before going on to a video book of direct images, the book finally being placed on the client's lap before browsed over. Finally, at the bedside, the person holds and feeds a spider in a jar's lid at home, takes it to sessions, and removes the jar in my presence, and releases the spider. I still seek to incorporate practice at a real-world level. I spent nearly 2 hours going up and down an elevator at the David Jones shop in Rundle Mall in Adelaide, with an old lady sticking to my top. We got strange looks from the detectives in the store! She was able to do it alone after about 2 hours, while I had coffee in a completely different shop 100 meters apart.

6. Self-talking: Help people describe what they communicate about themselves during periods of saying fear or distress, and record the precipitating triggers. That's where the above-mentioned journal or diary may be useful. The patients are then asked to write a better script or suggest more uplifting or positive

words about themselves during these periods. It is here that the theories of Albert Ellis (mentioned above) can be useful. He points out that by catastrophizing and expecting too much from the world, we are making ourselves miserable. It's not sensible to expect everyone to love us. A failed dinner party is not really a "ghastly," "horrible," or "terrible" trivial matter! We should do what we can to make a bad situation better, but beyond that, we should be worried about wasting emotional energy.

Does everybody believe that CBT is good? No. No. Arthur Janov from the renowned "The primitive scream" (the 70s) saw such approaches as a result of a futile, shallow "let's get along" mentality that overlooked the inner truths, the psychological neurosis concomitant. In his Psychiatric Times article (July 2001), "On the Banality of Positive Thinking," Simon Sobo sees CBT as a symptom of economic rationalism, and the whole "cookie-cutter" treatment fits all psychological diagnostic and treatment approaches. Again he maintains that the realities of the patient are ignored. Yet one doesn't have to fully ignore all behavioral counseling principles. It would be a big mistake to cast the baby out with the bathwater. For example, dismissing the importance of symbolism would be a massive mistake merely because symbolism is a feature of Freudian and Jungian psychology. We use "livestock" as an emblem. They are representations of those particular words. Symbolism psychology is not alien to stimulus-response psychology, as it is precisely through reinforcement processes that things and events acquire their symbolic value.

CPSIA information can be obtained
at www.ICGtesting.com
Printed in the USA
BVHW092358280121
599006BV00016B/1570